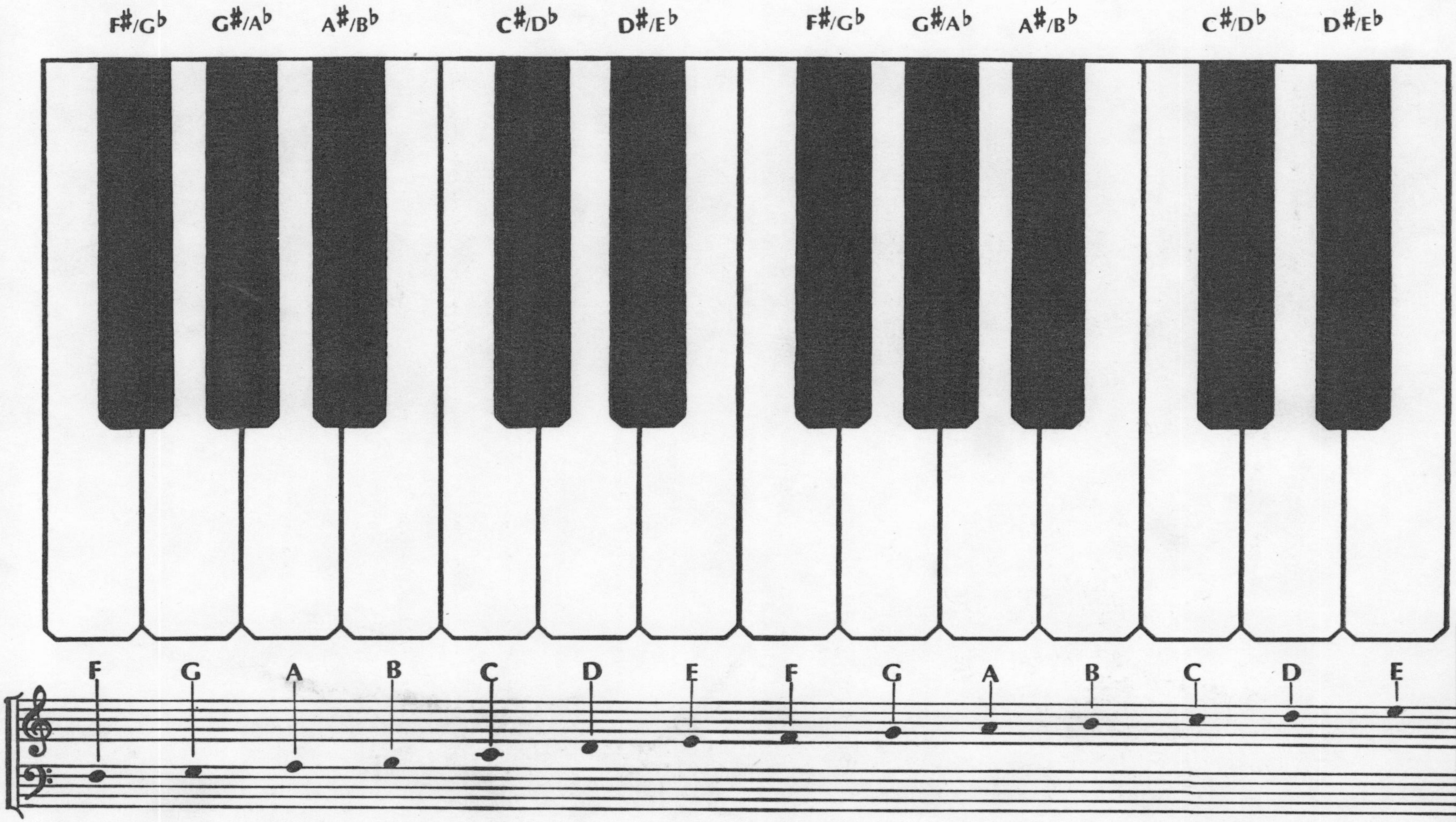
F#/Gb
G#/Ab
A#/Bb
C#/Db
D#/Eb
F#/Gb
G#/Ab
A#/Bb
C#/Db
D#/Eb
F
G
A
B
C
D
E
F
G
A
B
C
D
E

World of Music

Carmen E. Culp • Lawrence Eisman

Mary E. Hoffman
Authors

Carmino Ravosa • Phyllis Weikart
Theme Musical   Movement

Darrell Bledsoe
Producer, Vocal Recordings

Silver Burdett & Ginn

Morristown, NJ • Needham, MA

Atlanta, GA • Cincinnati, OH • Dallas, TX • Menlo Park, CA • Deerfield, IL

ISBN 0-382-07051-8

Contents

Music for Living 2

Understanding Music 54

Sharing Music 156

THEME MUSICAL – I LIKE MUSIC 204

Sing and Celebrate 216

Reference Bank

MUSIC FOR LIVING

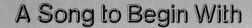

A Song to Begin With

Music is an almost magical thing. What is it about music that makes it so powerful?

Why do people sing? Often, of course, we sing simply because we are glad to be alive and singing. Here is a lighthearted song about a new day beginning.

It's a Good Day

Words and Music by Peggy Lee and Dave Barbour

Guitar:

Yes, it's a good day ___ for sing-in' a song, ___ and it's a

good day ___ for mov-in' a - long. ___ Yes, it's a good day, ___

___ how could an - y-thing go wrong, A good day from morn-in' till night. ___

___ Yes, it's a good day ___ for shin-in' your shoes, ___ And it's a

good day ___ for los-in' the blues, ___ Ev-'ry-thing to gain and

no-thin' to lose __'cause it's a good day from morn-in' till night. _____

I said to the sun, __ "Good morn-in', Sun, _ rise and shine to-day. ___

You know you've got-ta get go-in' if you're gon-na make a

show-in', and you know you've got the right of way." ✳ 'Cause it's a

good day ___ for wear-in' a grin, ___ and it's a good day ___ for

play-in' to win, ___ So take a deep breath, ___ and let it all be-

1.
gin, 'cause it's a good day from morn-in' till night. _____ I

2.
good day from morn-in', such a good day from morn-in' till night. _____

A Singing World

Since the beginning of time, people have used singing to express joy or sadness. Songs are sung in gratitude for a good harvest or to comfort people in hard times. Songs can give us courage when we are afraid or express our excitement when something wonderful happens.

Songs can tell about love—love for a person, love for a homeland. Songs can express faith and hope, and songs can turn away despair.

We sing to entertain ourselves and to share music with others. We sing to tell stories and to make musical jokes.

We sing songs that pass along the heritage of our ancestors. We sing songs of praise and worship and songs that help us celebrate special days.

A Song for the River

A song can be used to promote an idea. What is the message of "A Friend of Mine"?

A Friend of Mine

Words and Music by Lorre Wyatt

Call and Response:

The 1. riv-er is, *the riv-er is,* The riv-er is, *the riv-er is,* The
2. moun-tain
3. o-cean

riv-er — is — a friend — of mine. And when I'm good, *and when I'm good,*

It treats me good, *it treats me good.* And when I'm bad, *and when I'm bad,*

It treats me bad, *it treats me bad.* It took a long time for me to find —

The les-son that I need-ed to learn, that if I'm good; If I'm good to the

riv-er, — If I'm good; if I'm good to the riv-er, —

If I'm good to the riv-er, — the riv-er will be good to me! —

A Storyteller's Song

Sometimes we *sing* a story instead of telling it.

The writer of this song tells a true story. The grandfather who sailed to America was a real person, all the places exist, and the events in the song really happened.

Away to America

Words and Music by Linda Williams

Guitar:

1. My grand-fa-ther jour-neyed, like so man-y oth-ers, he turned to the West and the
heard of the moun-tains in far Col-o-ra-do, where ea-gles flew free in the

all he took with him was what he could car-ry, his books and an old vi-o-
moth-er was born there not man-y years af-ter, and all of her sis-ters as

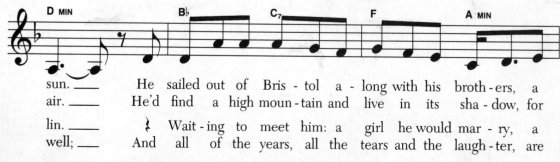

sun. _____ He sailed out of Bris-tol a-long with his broth-ers, a
air. _____ He'd find a high moun-tain and live in its sha-dow, for
lin. _____ 𝄽 Wait-ing to meet him: a girl he would mar-ry, a
well; _____ And all of the years, all the tears and the laugh-ter, are

1.
D MIN   A MIN   D MIN   G

new world was there to be won.
new life a-bout to be-gin.

2.
D MIN7   G7   G MIN7   C7

He'd some-thing was call-ing him there. _
My there in the stor-ies they tell. _

REFRAIN

F   A MIN   Bb7   C7   F   A MIN   Bb7   C7

"Sail a-way, a-way to A-mer-i-ca, Far off o-ver the sea.

D MIN   D MIN7   G MIN7   F   G MIN7   C7   D MIN   D.S.

There is some-thing there in A-mer-i-ca, And it's call-ing to me. 2. Now

3. Now I've gone away, there was nothing to hold me,
I flew off to London and stayed.
But still I remember the stories they told me,
And think of the journey he made.
Now I miss the mountains when I look around me,
And I really can't tell you when,
But somehow the voice of my grandfather found me
And soon I'll be flying again.
Fly away, come home to America . . .

Sail away . . .

An International Heritage

The people of America can trace their cultural heritage to every nation of the world. One person might be able to say, "I am part French, part Russian, part English, and part Navajo!" Another might say, "I am a first-generation American. All my ancestors come from China." Americans come in many varieties. Our music, too, is a rich mixture of international styles.

A Song from Scotland

"Bonnie Doon" was written about 1788. The music is traditional, and the words are by the famous Scottish poet Robert Burns.

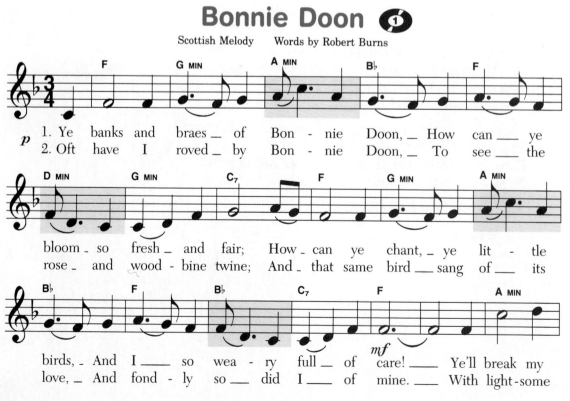

Bonnie Doon

Scottish Melody   Words by Robert Burns

p

1. Ye banks and braes _ of Bon - nie Doon, _ How can _ ye
2. Oft have I roved _ by Bon - nie Doon, _ To see _ the

bloom _ so fresh _ and fair; How _ can ye chant, _ ye lit - tle
rose _ and wood - bine twine; And _ that same bird _ sang of _ its

birds, _ And I ___ so wea - ry full _ of care! ___ Ye'll break my
love, _ And fond - ly so _ did I ___ of mine. ___ With light-some

10

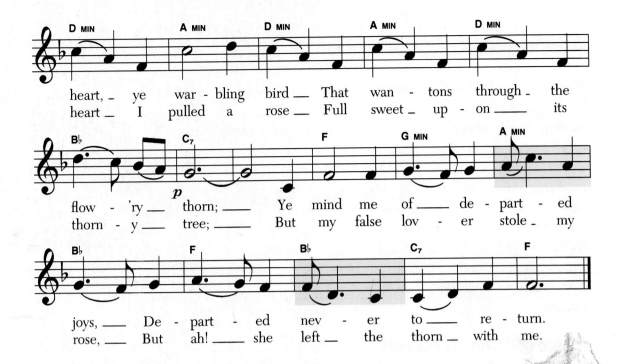

heart, ye war-bling bird That wan-tons through the
heart I pulled a rose Full sweet up-on its

flow-'ry thorn; Ye mind me of de-part-ed
thorn-y tree; But my false lov-er stole my

joys, De-part-ed nev-er to re-turn.
rose, But ah! she left the thorn with me.

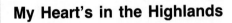

My Heart's in the Highlands

My heart's in the Highlands, my heart is not here;
My heart's in the Highlands a-chasing the deer;
A-chasing the wild deer, and following the roe—
My heart's in the Highlands wherever I go.

Farewell to the Highlands, farewell to the North,
The birthplace of valor, the country of worth:
Wherever I wander, wherever I rove,
The hills of the Highlands forever I love.

Farewell to the mountains high-covered with snow;
Farewell to the straths and green valleys below;
Farewell to the forests and wild-hanging woods;
Farewell to the torrents and loud-pouring floods.

My heart's in the Highlands . . . .

Robert Burns

11

A Song from Down Under

The most famous of Australian songs is "Waltzing Matilda."
It is the story of a "swagman" who runs afoul of the law and
drowns in a "billabong." The song is full of Australian slang.

Waltzing Matilda

Words by A. B. Patterson   Music by Maria Cowan

1. Once a jol - ly swag - man sat be - side the bil - la - bong,
2. Down ___ came a jum - buck to drink be - side the bil - la - bong,

Un - der the shade of a coo - li - bah tree, And he
Up jumped the swag - man and seized him with glee, And he

sang as he sat and wait - ed till his bil - ly boiled,
sang as he talked to that jum - buck in his tuck - er - bag,

"You'll come a - waltz - ing, Ma - til - da, with me."
"You'll come a - waltz - ing, Ma - til - da, with me."

REFRAIN

Waltz - ing Ma - til - da, waltz - ing Ma - til - da,
Waltz - ing Ma - til - da, waltz - ing Ma - til - da,

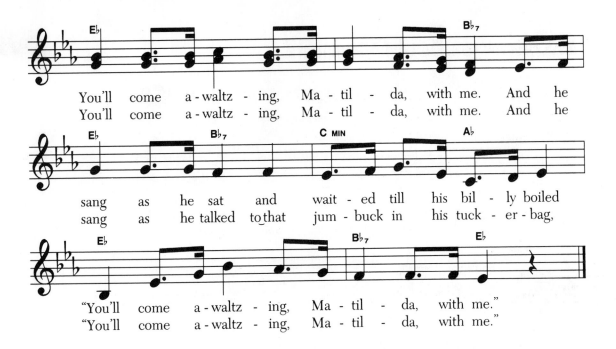

You'll come a-waltz-ing, Ma-til-da, with me. And he
You'll come a-waltz-ing, Ma-til-da, with me. And he

sang as he sat and wait-ed till his bil-ly boiled
sang as he talked to that jum-buck in his tuck-er-bag,

"You'll come a-waltz-ing, Ma-til-da, with me."
"You'll come a-waltz-ing, Ma-til-da, with me."

3. Down came the stockman, riding on his thoroughbred,
Down came the troopers, one, two, three.
"Where's the jolly jumbuck you've got in your tuckerbag?
You'll come a-waltzing, Matilda, with me." *Refrain*

4. Up jumped the swagman and plunged into the billabong,
"You'll never catch me alive," cried he;
And his ghost may be heard as you ride beside the billabong,
"You'll come a-waltzing, Matilda, with me." *Refrain*

Australian songs tend to be good-natured, easygoing, and often humorous. Even rock bands from Australia like to play songs that are full of mischief.

"Down Under" . . . . Men at Work

Two Songs about Moonlight

Serenade *(Lu Lépre)*

Traditional Italian Song   English Version by Bella Giovanni

Soft - ly the wind ___ in the for - est is blow - ing
Sof - fia il ven - to e splen - de la lu - na,

through the trees ___ and the pale moon is glow - ing. ___
sbri - ga - ti che non si ve - de nes - su - no. ___

Soft as the wind ___ and pale as the moon, you'll not see my face ___
Sof - fia il ven - to splen - de la lu - na fer - ma - ti ___

— nor hear my go - ing. ___
— che cé qual - cu - no. ___

In the Moonlight *(Au clair de la lune)*

Traditional French Song   English Version by D. Auberge

Stand - ing in the moon - light, Mon a - mi Pier - rot,
Au clair de la lu - ne, Mon a - mi Pier - rot,

I have lost my can - dle, How, I do not know!
Prê - te - moi ta plu - me, Pour é - crire un mot;

14

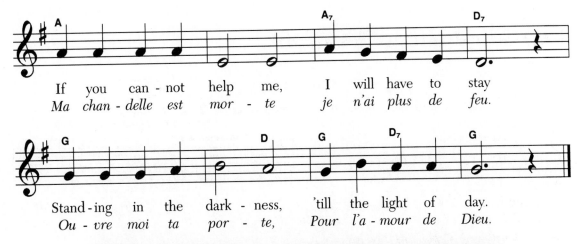

If you can-not help me, I will have to stay
Ma chan-delle est mor - te je n'ai plus de feu.

Stand-ing in the dark-ness, 'till the light of day.
Ou - vre moi ta por - te, Pour l'a-mour de Dieu.

Carnival Evening
Henri Rousseau

From Eastern Europe

A Song of Freedom

Waters Ripple and Flow

Slovokian Folk Song   English Words by Marta Novak

1. Wa - ters rip - ple and flow, ___ Rush - ing swift - ly from
2. Faith as strong as the riv - er, Cour - age wide ___ as the
3. Riv - er swift - ly flow - ing Heed my yearn - ing ___

me. 'Cross the land ___ I love,
sea. For the land ___ I love,
heart. Some - day I will re - turn,

Run - ning on ___ to the sea. 'Cross the land ___ I
For the right _ to be free. For the land ___ I
Ne - ver to ___ de - part. Some - day I will re -

love, Run - ning on ___ to the sea.
love, For the right ___ to be free.
turn, Ne - ver to ___ de - part.

A Song for Selling Fine Clothes

The Peddler *(Korobushka)*

Russian Folk Song   English Words Adapted by Linda Williams

1. Treas - ures have I in my Ko - ro - bush - ka, ___
2. Cost - ly and fine are the wares I bring you, ___
3. Treas - ures have I in my Ko - ro - bush - ka, ___

Can you hear the pedd - ler's cry?
Love - ly la - dy, feast your eye!
Bring your ko - pecks, come and buy!

REFRAIN

{ Though you see me in rags and tat - ters I
You may dance to the ba - la - lai - ka ___

wear a smile up - on my face.
wear - ing sa - tin, silk, and lace.

After you learn the song, you can add this countermelody.

La la la la, La la la la, La la la la, La la la la.

La la la la, La la la la, La la la la la la la.

17

Songs of Israel

Around the Campfire

"Finjan" is the Turkish word for coffee pot.

Finjan

Israeli Campfire Song

A cool des - ert wind blow - ing by,
Ha - ru - ach no - she - vet k'ri - rah,

the wood on the
No - sif od ki -

fire burn - ing high,
sam lam - du - rah;

We sit in the flick - er - ing
Ve - kach biz ro - ot ar - ga -

light
man,

and send out our song to the night.
va - esh ya - a - leh ke - kor - ban;

The song will re - sound as we pass it a - round, as we
Ha - esh me - hav - he - vet, shir - a me lav le - vet so -

pass it a - round, ha - fin - jan
vev lo so - vev ha - fin - jan.

La la la la la la

la la la la la la la la la la la la la la,   La la la

la la la la   la la la la   The song will re - sound as we
Ha - esh me - hav - he - vet, shir -

pass it a - round, as we pass it a - round, ha - fin - jan.
a me - lav lev - et so - vev lo so - vev ha - fin - jan.

This tambourine part will go with the "La la la" section:

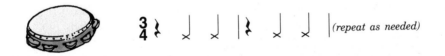

(repeat as needed)

Yibane Amenu

Round from Israel

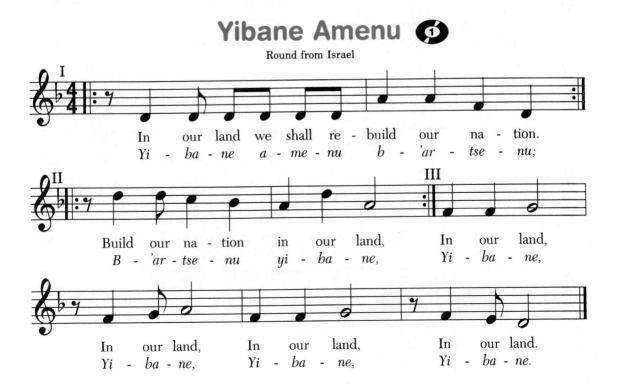

In   our   land   we   shall   re - build   our   na - tion.
Yi - ba - ne   a - me - nu   b - 'ar - tse - nu;

Build   our   na - tion   in   our   land,   In   our   land,
B - 'ar - tse - nu   yi - ba - ne,   Yi - ba - ne,

In   our   land,   In   our   land,   In   our   land.
Yi - ba - ne,   Yi - ba - ne,   Yi - ba - ne.

From the Far East

A Song from Okinawa

Okinawa is a Pacific Island nation,
but the culture and language are
Japanese. This love song from
Okinawa is in the Japanese style.

Asadoya

Folk Song from Okinawa

1. Ah, House of As - a - do - ya __ Why are you so dear to __
2. A - las __ fair Ku - ya - ma, __ Cru - el, o cru - el was
3. Lo! now __ I have wed an - oth - er. Fair - er by far than __
4. And if __ she bear me a son, __ Rul - er of this town he will

me? Sa yu - i yu - i 'Tis where ku - ya - ma
she, Sa yu - i yu - i Cold - ly dis - dain - ing me,
thee. Sa yu - i yu - i With grace - ful man - ners fine,
be; Sa yu - i yu - i And if a daugh - ter fair, A

first the light of day __ did __ see. And she was my love, my
She re - fused my bride __ to __ be. And she was my love, my
Dwell we now in hap - py har - mo - ny, And she is my love, my
mo - del of __ sweet fe - li - ci - ty, And she'll be my love, my

dar - ling and all the world to me. _____
dar - ling and all the world to me. _____
dar - ling and all the world to me. _____
dar - ling and all the world to me. _____

20

Fantasy on Japanese Woodprints (excerpt)........
.............................Alan Hovhaness

River-Fog

Because the river-fog
Hiding the mountain base
Has risen,
The autumn mountain looks as though it hung in the sky.

—Fukayabu Kiyowara
translated by Authur Waley

Music from Mexico

Here is a song that can be sung for birthdays, or just as a "morning song." Try singing it in two parts.

Las mañanitas

Mexican Folk Song   English Version by Lupe Allegria

Hear us sing las ma - ña - ni - tas, as the
Es - tas son las ma - ña - ni - tas, Que can -

morn - ing light ap - pears, And the gen - tle bird will
ta - ba el Rey Da - vid, A las mu - cha - chas bo -

join in the hap - py mu - sic he hears. Oh,
ni - tas Se las can - ta - mos a - quí. Des -

wake up and see the sun - shine. Oh, wake up and meet the
pier - ta, mi bien, des - pier - ta, Mi - ra que ya a - man - ne -

day. Hear, the morn - ing bird is sing - ing, the sil - ver
ció; Ya los pa - ja - ri - llos can - tan, La lu - na

moon has gone a - way.
ya ___ se me - tió.

A "charro" is a peasant or a farmhand. This charro is not well-thought-of by his foreman!

El charro

Mexican Folk Song

1. There was a *char-ro* a-sit-ting_____ on the fence of a
2. "I need a horse and a sad-dle_____ and some boots and a

1. (Repeat each verse) **2.**

wide cor-ral._____ —
coat of red."_____

Then came his fore-man to
Kind-ly the fore-man as-

ask him,_____ "Why so mourn-ful, Ni-co-lás?"_____
sured him,_____ "You shall have them, Ni-co-lás!"_____

3. "Just one more thing," said *el charro,* ⎫ *repeat*
   "I would marry your daughter, too," ⎭
   Firmly the foreman assured him, ⎫ *repeat*
   "She is taken, Nicolás!" ⎭

4. *El charro* cried out, despairing, ⎫ *repeat*
   "I will throw myself off the cliff!" ⎭
   Kindly the foreman suggested, ⎫ *repeat*
   "Then go head first, Nicolás!" ⎭

23

A Calypso Song

Calypso songs originated many years ago in the West Indies.
Plantation slaves were often forbidden to talk, so they sang
the news and gossip to one another in rhythmic song patterns
as they worked.

Hold 'em, Joe

Words and Music by Harry Thomas

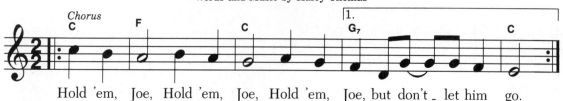

Hold 'em, Joe, Hold 'em, Joe, Hold 'em, Joe, but don't _ let him go.

Joe, but don't _ let him go. Me don - key want wa - ter, Hold 'em, Joe;

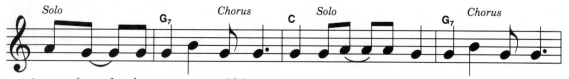

Spring 'round _ the cor - ner, Hold 'em, Joe; Me don - key want wa - ter, Hold 'em,

Joe; Ev - 'ry - bo - dy want wa - ter, Hold 'em, Joe; Fu - ma - la - ca tchim - ba,

Hold 'em, Joe; Me don - key want wa - ter, Hold 'em Joe; Ev - 'ry - bo - dy want

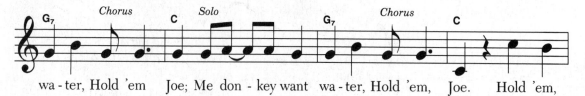

wa - ter, Hold 'em Joe; Me don - key want wa - ter, Hold 'em, Joe. Hold 'em,

A Sad Goodbye

Here is another song from the West Indies. The words are about saying goodbye to a place that will be sadly missed.

Jamaica Farewell

Words and Music by Lord Burgess

1. Down the way where the nights are gay ___ and the
2. Sounds of laugh - ter are ev - 'ry - where ___ and the

sun shines dai - ly on the moun - tain - top, ___
danc - ing girls ___ are sway - ing to and fro. ___

I took a trip on a sail - ing ship ___ and when I
I must de - clare that my heart is there ___ tho' I have

reached Ja - mai - ca I made a stop. ___ } But I'm
been from Maine ___ to old Mex - i - co. ___

sad to say I'm on my way, ___

Won't be back for man - y a day. ___ My

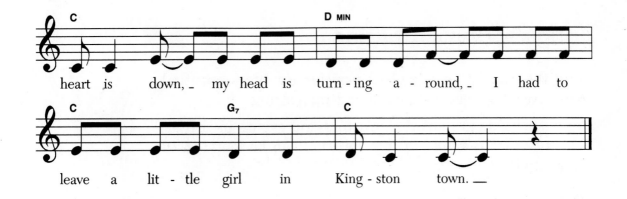

heart is down, _ my head is turn-ing a-round, _ I had to leave a lit-tle girl in King-ston town. _

This countermelody goes with the last four lines of the song.

Bells or Recorder:

Songs of Black America

Of all the music that is truly American, the black spirituals are among the most distinctive and interesting.

Many spirituals are about characters and events in the Bible. The story that is retold in this spiritual can be found in the Old Testament.

Didn't My Lord Deliver Daniel?

Black Spiritual

Did - n't   my Lord   de - liv - er   Dan - iel, ___ de - liv - er

Dan - iel, ___ de - liv - er   Dan - iel? ___ Did - n't   my Lord   de - liv - er

Dan - iel? ___ Then   why not - a   ev - er - y   man?   Did - n't

man?   1. He   de - liv - ered   Dan - iel from the   li - on's   den, _
        2. Oh   the wind blows East ___ and the   wind blows West _
        3. When the   moon runs   down ___ in   a   sil - ver   stream _

Jo - nah   from the   bel - ly   of   the   whale,   And   the
Blows __   like - a   judge - a - ment __   day,   And ___
Sun ___   will   re - fuse ___   to ___   shine,   And ___

28

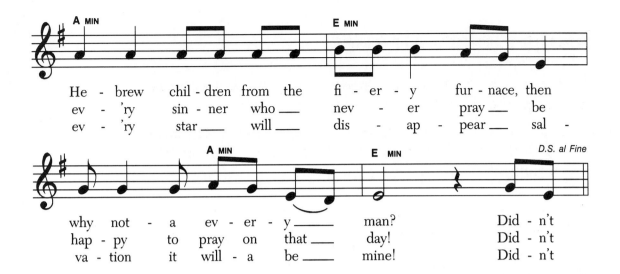

He - brew chil - dren from the fi - er - y fur - nace, then
ev - 'ry sin - ner who___ nev - er pray___ be
ev - 'ry star___ will___ dis - ap - pear___ sal -

D.S. al Fine

why not - a ev - er - y_____ man? Did - n't
hap - py to pray on that___ day! Did - n't
va - tion it will - a be_____ mine! Did - n't

Spirituals were invented by black Americans, but these songs
have become part of our national heritage. All Americans,
regardless of their ethnic background, love to sing spirituals.

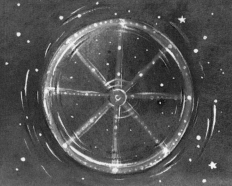

A Wheel in a Wheel

Ezekiel Saw the Wheel ②

Black Spiritual

E - ze - kiel _ saw the wheel, 'Way up in the mid - dle of the air,

E - ze - kiel _ saw the wheel, 'Way in the mid - dle of the air.

Now the big wheel turn by faith, And the lit - tle wheel turn by the

grace of God, It's a wheel in a wheel, 'Way in the mid - dle of the air.

1. Some go to church for to sing and shout, 'Way in the mid - dle of the air,
2. One of these _ days 'bout _ twelve o' - clock, 'Way in the mid - dle of the air,

Be - fore six months they're shout - ed out! 'Way in the mid - dle of the air. E -
{ This old world gonna reel and rock! 'Way in the mid - dle of the air. E -

30

Little Wheel A-Turnin' ②

Black Spiritual

1. There's a lit-tle wheel a-turn-in' in my heart, There's a
2. There's a lit-tle song a-sing-in' in my heart, There's a
3. There's a lit-tle love a-liv-in' in my heart, There's a

lit-tle wheel a-turn-in' in my heart; In my
lit-tle song a-sing-in' in my heart; In my
lit-tle love a-liv-in' in my heart; In my

heart, _____ in my heart. _____ There's a
heart, _____ in my heart. _____ There's a
heart, _____ in my heart. _____ There's a

lit-tle wheel a-turn-in' in my heart.
lit-tle song a-sing-in' in my heart.
lit-tle love a-liv-in' in my heart.

4. There's a little bell a-ringin' in my heart,

5. There's a little drum a-beatin' in my heart,

A Musical Code

Swing Low, Sweet Chariot 2

Black Spiritual

REFRAIN

Swing low, sweet char - i - ot, _____ Com - in' for to car - ry me home; Swing _ low, sweet char - i - ot, _____ Com - in' for to car - ry me home.

Fine VERSE

1. I looked o - ver Jor - dan and
2. If you get _ there _ be -
3. I'm some - times _ up, I'm _____

what did I _ see? _____ A
fore _ I _ do, _____ Com - in' for to car - ry me home; Tell
some - times _ down, _____ But

D.C. al Fine

band _ of an - gels com - in' af - ter me, _____
all _ my friends I'm com - in' _____ too, _____ Com - in' for to car - ry me home.
still _ my soul feels heav'n - ly _ bound, _

32

Let Me Fly

Black Spiritual

1. Way down yon-der in the mid-dle of the field,
2. I got a moth-er in the prom-ised _ land,
3. Meet that hyp-o-crite _ on _ the _ street,

An - gel work-in' on the char-iot wheel. Not so par-ti-cu-lar 'bout
Ain't gonna stop _ till I shake her hand. Not so par-ti-cu-lar 'bout
First thing he'll do _ is _ show his teeth. Next thing he'll do _ is _

work-in' at the wheel, But I just want-a see how the char-iot feels.
shak-in' her _ hand, But I just want-a go up to the prom-ised land.
tell _ a _ lie, And the best thing to do is _ pass him by.

REFRAIN

Now let me fly,_ (Now let me fly) Now let me fly,_ (Now

All:

let me fly) Now let me fly _ in - to Mount Zi - on,

Last time go on (All Clap)

Lord, Lord. _____

An American Indian Song

This song was written by two American Indian college students.

The music of the song is like some of the popular music we are used to hearing. However, the words echo the heritage of the songwriters. In the lyrics, they look to their tribal leaders for guidance and inspiration, as their people have for many centuries.

Go, My Son

Words and Music by Burson-Nofchissey

Spoken: *Long ago an Indian War Chief counseled his people in the way they should walk. He wisely told them that education is the ladder to success and happiness. "Go, my son, and climb that ladder. . . ."*

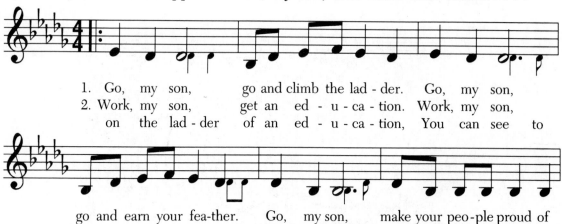

1. Go, my son, go and climb the lad-der. Go, my son,
2. Work, my son, get an ed-u-ca-tion. Work, my son,
   on the lad-der of an ed-u-ca-tion, You can see to

go and earn your fea-ther. Go, my son, make your peo-ple proud of
learn a good vo-ca-tion and Climb, my son, go and take a loft-y
help your In-dian na-tion and Reach, my son, and lift your peo-ple up with

1. you. _____
2. view. _____ 3. From
3. you. _____

34

Go,   my   son,   go and climb the lad - der,   Go,   my   son,
on   the   lad - der   of an ed - u - ca - tion,   You   can   see   to

Last time
to Coda

go   and earn your fea - ther.   Go   my   son,   make your peo - ple proud of
help your In - dian na - tion, then

Coda   *rit.*

you. _____ From   Reach, my son.   Lift your peo - ple up with you.

You can learn to perform "Go, My Son" in traditional Indian
Sign Language. Use the signs illustrated on the next page.

Here are the signs you can use as you sing the refrain of "Go, My Son."

climb

proud

good

vocation

of you

education

Indian

reach

Here is some traditional American Indian music. In this
example, the only tones we hear are the five notes of a
pentatonic scale.

 "Round Dance Song".............................
.... Traditional Taos Indian Music

Look at the melody of "Go, My Son." How is it similar?

Call Chart 1

2 *Sundance* . . . . Linda Williams

Here are some of the musical ideas that are used in *Sundance*.
There is even a theme made out of the composer's name.

1. A strong, heavy pattern of five beats:

2. A texture of strings, harp, bells and piano, all moving upward:

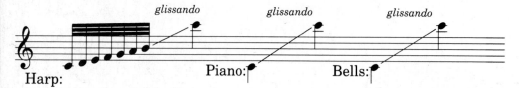

3. The recurring pattern of three notes, moving upward:

4. The "Sundance" theme, introduced by the trumpet:

5. Brass players creating the sound of the wind:

Blow through mouthpiece
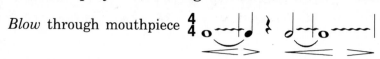

6. The "signature" theme, made out of the composer's name:

Music for the Mountain

Sundance is a small ski resort on Mount Timpanogos in Utah.
The American composer Linda Williams sketched the idea
for her piece one summer day at Sundance. She wanted to paint
a musical picture of the mountain.

Sundance . . . . Linda Williams

Linda Williams
(b. 1931)

Linda Williams has been writing music
all her life. As a music teacher she has
written hundreds of songs for her students, many of which have been published. She wrote "Away to America"
(page 8) for her students to sing.

She won a national prize for a set of
piano pieces while she was still a college
student, and she has been a working
composer since. Large orchestral pieces
like *Sundance* and small chamber works
are her favorite projects. She continues
to write many songs each year.

A Nation of Immigrants

The song "Away to America" on page 8 tells the story of one young man who came to America from the British Isles. Immigrants from many countries came to these shores, bringing their customs, their languages, and their songs.

An Immigrant's Son

American composer George Gershwin was the son of Russian-Jewish immigrants, who came to America before the turn of the century. He was born in Brooklyn in 1898 into a home with very little in the way of wealth or social standing. But he would become one of the most successful American composers of his time. George Gershwin was that American ideal, an immigrant's son who made good.

George Gershwin
(1898–1937)

George Gershwin's life was tragically short, but his impact on American music was great. He wrote songs like "I Got Rhythm," "Liza," "Strike Up the Band," and many others. They have become popular classics. He also wrote serious concert pieces, using the catchy melodies, jazzy harmonies, and driving rhythms of popular music.

You are probably familiar with some of Gershwin's concert pieces. They are played all over the world, and have been recorded many times by famous orchestras and concert artists.

His songs for the musical theater are among his most famous and best-loved pieces.

You may already have heard Gershwin's most famous work, *Rhapsody in Blue.* The opening clarinet *glissando* immediately announces that the piece will be full of jazz elements.

 Rhapsody in Blue (excerpt) . . . . Gershwin

In *An American in Paris,* Gershwin drew a musical picture of a visitor to Paris walking the busy streets.

 An American in Paris (excerpts) . . . . Gershwin

All the songs in this medley are from famous Broadway shows by George Gershwin.

 Medley ("Of Thee I Sing," "Liza," "Strike Up the Band"). . . . . George Gershwin

George Gershwin—Boyhood Years

When George was twelve years old, a piano was brought into
his home. It was meant for his older brother Ira, who was to
begin piano lessons. But George surprised everyone by picking
out songs on the piano, some even with his own catchy
accompaniments.

About that time he heard the music of songwriter Irving Berlin.
"This is American music," he said, "This is the kind of music
I want to write."

 "Alexander's Ragtime Band" . . . . Irving Berlin

Among the tunes he may have played on the piano were
popular songs like "Waiting for the Robert E. Lee." This lively,
syncopated minstrel-style song was popular when George
Gershwin was about fourteen years old.

Waiting for the Robert E. Lee

Words by Lewis F. Muir   Music by L. Wolfe Gilbert

While we are wait - in,' the ban-jos are syn - co - pa - tin'.

That's come to car - ry the cot - ton a - way.

See them step - pin' a - long;

Hear us sing - in' a - long. Go take your best gal, real

pal, Go down by the lev - ee, I said to the lev - ee! And then

join that ju - bi-lant throng, Hear that mu - sic and song:

It's sim - ply great, mate, Wait-in' on the lev - ee,

Wait - in' for the Rob - ert E. Lee!

The Song Plugger

At the age of fifteen, Gershwin left high school to take a job as a "song plugger." When Gershwin was twenty, he was given a job writing songs for a publisher.

His first "hit" was a song called "Swanee," written in 1919. It sold over two million records.

Swanee

Words by Irving Caesar   Music by George Gershwin

Swan - ee,   How I love you, How I love you, My   dear old Swan - ee; ___

I'd give the world   to   be   A - mong the folks   in   D - I - X - I -

E - ven now there's some   -   one   Wait - ing for me, Pray - ing for me

Down   by   the   Swan - ee, ___ The folks up   north   will

see me no more ___ When I get to the Swan - ee   shore. ___

George Gershwin, Pianist

In addition to being one of America's foremost composer-songwriters, George Gershwin was an accomplished pianist.

Listen to this old recording of George Gershwin playing his version of one of his songs.

 "I Got Rhythm" .... Gershwin

Gershwin also wrote serious works for piano.

Call Chart 2

Listen to these piano preludes from three different centuries. Notice how they are alike and how they are different.

1. Even rhythms, broken chords, regular harmony changes

 "Prelude No. 1" from *The Well Tempered Clavier* .. ..Bach

2. Thick texture, rich harmony

Prelude Op. 28 No. 20..................... Chopin

3. Rhythms and harmonies often found in jazz, melody in the style of popular music.

"Prelude No. 1" from *Three Piano Preludes* ....Gershwin

Porgy and Bess, An American Opera

George Gershwin's opera *Porgy and Bess* is considered by many to be his finest work.

The story of the opera takes place in Catfish Row, a waterfront tenement section of Charleston, South Carolina. It tells how Porgy, a crippled black beggar, finds Bess, falls in love with her, and loses her to another man. She has been lured away to New York, and Porgy is determined to find her. The final scene shows Porgy setting out hopefully to bring her home.

One of the most famous songs in the opera is this lullaby.

Summertime ③

Words by Dubose Heyward   Music by George Gershwin

Sum-mer-time ____ And the liv-in' is eas-y, ____ Fish are

jump-in', ____ And the cot-ton is high. ____ Oh, your dad-dy's rich ____

____ And your ma is good-look-in', ____ So hush, lit-tle ba-by, don't _ you

cry. ____ One of these morn-in's ____ You goin' to rise _ up sing-in', _

____ Then you'll spread your wings _ And you'll take _ the sky. ___ But till that

morn - in' _____ There's - a noth - in' can harm you _____ With

Dad - dy and Mam - my stand - in' by. _____

Call Chart 3

Concerto in F, Themes from Movement 3 . . . . Gershwin

1. (A)   etc.

2. (Concerto theme)   ((A) comes from this theme)   etc.

3. [B]   etc.

   and   etc.

4. (C)   etc.

5. Variation of (A)   etc.

6. Another (A)   etc.

7. Coda

Concerto in F, Movement 3 . . . . Gershwin

A Famous Gershwin Song

One of his most famous songs for Broadway, this song was written for a 1930 show called *Girl Crazy*.

I Got Rhythm

Words by Ira Gershwin   Music by George Gershwin

Test 1

Here are descriptions of several of the folk songs in your book. The songs come from many nations, but have many elements in common. Each has a distinctive style and purpose, however. Match the descriptions with the songs, and write the letter in the blank.

1. A song that is like a singing commercial for clothing _____

2. A song that imitates flowing water _____

3. A song about a stubborn donkey _____

4. A song haunted by a ghost _____

5. A song sung by a robber _____

6. A song with words by a famous poet _____

7. A song about fireside companionship _____

8. A comedy song about a fieldhand _____

9. A song with a tune using only five tones _____

10. A sad goodbye song _____

Use your index to find these songs if you need to look at them.

A. Finjan
B. Bonnie Doon
C. Waltzing Matilda
D. Jamaica Farewell
E. Asadoya

F. Serenade
G. Waters Ripple and Flow
H. The Peddler
I. El charro
J. Hold 'Em, Joe

50

What Do You Hear 1

You will hear eight pieces for instruments. Each will be in the *style* of a song in your book, even though the music is different from that song. Circle the title of the song you think is *most like* the music you hear.

LISTENING SKILLS 3 *Styles Montage*

1. "Hold 'em, Joe"   "Serenade"

2. "Swing Low, Sweet Chariot"   "Waltzing Matilda"

3. "Waters Ripple and Flow"   "El charro"

4. "It's a Good Day"   "Asadoya"

5. "Las mañanitas"   "Bonnie Doon"

6. "Didn't My Lord Deliver Daniel?"   "In the Moonlight"

7. "Bonnie Doon"   "It's a Good Day"

8. "In the Moonlight"   "A Friend of Mine"

Test 2 ✓

Here are five descriptions of musical selections you have listened to. After each description are two choices of titles. Circle the title of the listening selection that fits the description.

1. A piano piece in a traditional form, with jazzy harmonies

Men At Work: "Down Under"   Gershwin: *Prelude*

2. A piece that spells the composer's name

Gershwin: *Concerto in F*   Williams: *Sundance*

3. A piano piece from the 1700s

Bach: "Prelude"   Gershwin: "I Got Rhythm"

4. A piece that describes a street scene

Gershwin: *Rhapsody in Blue*   Gershwin: *An American in Paris*

5. Music built on a five-tone scale

Hovhaness: *Fantasy on Japanese Woodprints*   Chopin: *Prelude*

What Do You Hear ? 2

Songs often create a mood. Usually the words are an important factor. However, music alone, even without words, can create a mood. You will hear eight instrumental accompaniments for songs in your book. Circle the words that best describe the mood of the music. You may choose one or more words.

 Moods Montage

1. Lively   Sad   Angry   Playful   Dreamy   Cheerful

2. Lively   Sad   Angry   Playful   Dreamy   Cheerful

3. Lively   Sad   Angry   Playful   Dreamy   Cheerful

4. Lively   Sad   Angry   Playful   Dreamy   Cheerful

5. Lively   Sad   Angry   Playful   Dreamy   Cheerful

6. Lively   Sad   Angry   Playful   Dreamy   Cheerful

7. Lively   Sad   Angry   Playful   Dreamy   Cheerful

8. Lively   Sad   Angry   Playful   Dreamy   Cheerful

Musical Interaction

Tone Color

RHYTHM

Harmony....+

Melody

FORM

STYLES

A

C

A

B

A

Rhythm—The Heartbeat of Music

When you find yourself tapping your foot to a piece of music, you are responding to rhythm. It is the heartbeat of music.

As you sing "Dinah," tap your hands on your knees or on your desk. Tap each time you see an x above the note. This is the *beat* of the music.

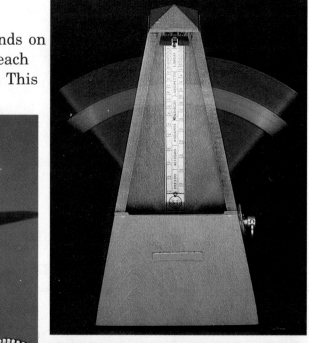

Dinah

Words by Sam M. Lewis and Joe Young   **Music by Harry Akst**

Din - ah, _____ is there an - y - one fin - er _____ In the state of Car - o -
Din - ah, _____ with her Dix - ie eyes blaz - in', _____ How I love to sit and

lin - a _____ If there is and you know her, show her to me? _
gaze in -

- to the eyes of Din - ah Lee. _____ Ev - 'ry night _ why do I _

shake with fright? _ Be - cause my Din - ah might _ change her mind _ a - bout

me. _____ Din - ah, _____ if she wan - dered to Chin - a, _____

I would hop an o - cean lin - er, _____ just to be with Din - ah Lee. _____

Tap to another version of "Dinah." Keep tapping even during
the silences. Keep the beat steady.

 "Dinah" Version 2

When the music stopped and then started again, were you
still on the right beat?

Tempo

Here are two short songs, both in $\frac{2}{4}$ meter. The *tempo,* or rate of speed, is the same for both songs. They can even be sung together, as "partner songs."

Early One Morning

English Folk Song

1. Ear - ly one morn - ing, be - fore the sun had ris - en,
2. One au - tumn af - ter - noon, just as the sun was set - ting,

I heard a blue - bird in the fields __ gai - ly sing,
I heard a blue - bird on a tree __ pipe a song,

"South winds are blow - ing, Green grass is grow - ing,
"Fare - well! We're go - ing, Cold winds are blow - ing,

We __ come to her - ald the mer - ry __ spring."
But __ we'll be back __ when the days __ grow __ long."

When you sing them together, the quarter note beat must be steady, even though one song seems to move faster.

Summer Night, Winter Night

Words and Music by Jean Riddle

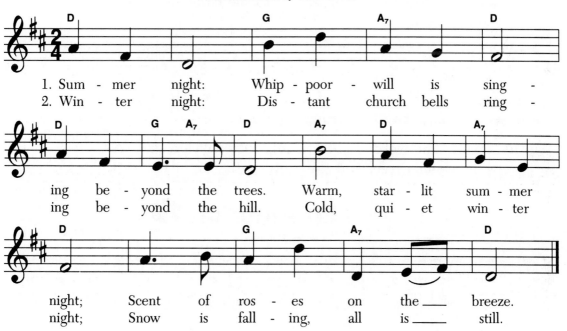

1. Sum - mer night: Whip - poor - will is sing -
2. Win - ter night: Dis - tant church bells ring -

ing be - yond the trees. Warm, star - lit sum - mer
ing be - yond the hill. Cold, qui - et win - ter

night; Scent of ros - es on the ___ breeze.
night; Snow is fall - ing, all is ___ still.

Listen to this piece for orchestra. The tempo stays the same, but the first part sounds faster than the second part.

LISTENING SKILLS 3 **Overture from** *Candide* **(excerpt)** .... **Bernstein**

Rhythm and Meter—Mixing Sixes

Begin with a group of six notes.

They can be divided up in a number of ways.

1.   2.

Accents help divide notes into rhythm patterns.

1.   2.

Play the first pattern on a drum. Play the second pattern on the claves. Have two players play the two patterns together.

The division of patterns is even easier to see when the eighth note is the beat note.

1.   2.

Sometimes music in a pattern of six will alternate between accenting groups of two and groups of three.

Try this chant. The words fall naturally into rhythm patterns in groups of two or three, and they alternate.

Latin America

Mary Hoffman

La - tin   A - mer - i - ca,   Con - ga, Tan - go, Mam - bo,   Mex - i - co,   E - cua - dor,

Chi - le, Cos - ta   Ri - ca,   Ur - u - guay, Par - a - guay,   Pe - ru,   Ar - gen - ti - na,

Sal - va - dor, Pan - a - ma,   Con - ga, Tan - go, Mam - bo,   La - tin   A - mer - i - ca!

In the musical play *West Side Story,* there is a song about Puerto Ricans living in New York City. This song uses the alternating three and two pattern of our chant.

 "America" from *West Side Story* .... Bernstein

Another Way to Mix Twos and Threes

A dance from *Carmina Burana* by Carl Orff also mixes two and threes. However, this time they occur in irregular patterns. The music begins this way:

Try clapping the rhythm pattern, then listen to the way it happens in the music.

 "Tanz" from *Carmina Burana* .... Orff

Rhythm Patterns—Divide and Conquer

Begin with a steady beat.
Tap your knees in a steady *quarter-note* rhythm.

Now tap a steady *eighth-note* rhythm. Alternate hands.

We have divided the beat in half. We can also divide each beat in half again. Tap this *sixteenth-note* rhythm.

Put it all together in order to hear the relationship better.

Drum:

Woodblock:

Tap:

Use a football chant to divide the quarter note. For the steady beat, say:

pass *pass*

Divide the beat. Say:

tack - le

Divide it again. Say:

in - ter - fer - ence

The beat can also be divided in other ways. We can combine eighth-note and sixteenth-note patterns.

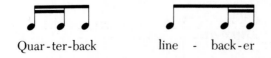

Quar-ter-back   line - back-er

Mister Touchdown, U. S. A. ④

Words and Music by Ruth Roberts, Gene Piller, and William Katz

They al-ways call him Mis-ter Touch-down, ___ They al-ways

call him Mis-ter Team. ___ He can run ___ and

kick and throw. ___ Give him the ball ___ and just look at him go. ___

___ Hip, hip, hoo-ray for Mis-ter Touch-down. ___

He's gon-na beat 'em to-day. ___ So give a great big cheer for the

he-ro of the year, Mis-ter Touch-down, U. S. A. ___

After you listen to "Mister Touchdown, U.S.A.," you can make
up a football chant to accompany it.

A Bell Song with Divided Beats

The very first line of "Ring, Bells" demonstrates one of
the patterns of beat division we have been learning about.

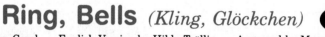

Single beat: Divided beat: Divided again

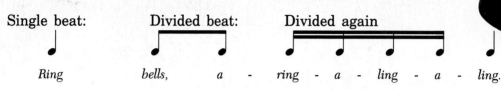

Ring   bells,   a - ring - a - ling - a - ling.

Ring, Bells *(Kling, Glöckchen)* 4

Traditional German Carol   English Version by Hilda Trällin   Arranged by Mary Hoffman

Ring,   bells,   a - ring - a - ling - a - ling,   Ring   lit - tle bells.
Kling,   Glöck - chen, kling - e - ling - e - ling,   Kling,   Glöck - chen, kling.

"O - pen, let us en - ter,   Cold the wind in win - ter."
Lasst mich ein ihr Kin - der,   Ist so kalt der Win - ter.

Maid and in - fant ho - ly,   In a room so low - ly.
Öff - net mir die Tür - en,   Lasst mich nicht er - frie - ren.

64

"Carillon" from *L'Arlésienne
Suite* (excerpt) . . . . Bizet

LISTENING
SKILLS
4

An Off-Beat Song

Play this tune on bells or piano. The strongest note is where we expect it.

Now play this version. This rhythmic device—accented notes in unexpected places—is called *syncopation*.

Comedy Tonight

Words and Music by Stephen Sondheim

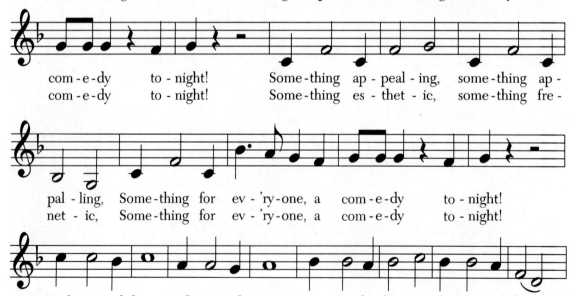

1. Some-thing fa-mil-iar, some-thing pe-cul-iar, Some-thing for ev-'ry-one, a
2. Some-thing con-vul-sive, some-thing re-pul-sive, Some-thing for ev-'ry-one, a

com-e-dy to-night! Some-thing ap-peal-ing, some-thing ap-
com-e-dy to-night! Some-thing es-thet-ic, some-thing fre-

pal-ling, Some-thing for ev-'ry-one, a com-e-dy to-night!
net-ic, Some-thing for ev-'ry-one, a com-e-dy to-night!

Noth-ing with kings, noth-ing with crowns. Bring on the lov-ers, li-ars, and clowns! _
Noth-ing of gods, noth-ing of fate. Weight-y af-fairs will just have to wait. _

Old sit - u - a - tions, new com - pli - ca - tions, Noth - ing por - ten - tous or po - lite; —
Noth - ing that's for - mal, noth - ing that's nor - mal, No rec - i - ta - tions to re - cite! —

— Trag - e - dy to - mor - row, com - e - dy to - night!
— O - pen up the cur - tains, com - e - dy to - night!

Tying It Together

Sometimes syncopation is created with *ties*.

Circles ④

Words and Music by Linda Williams

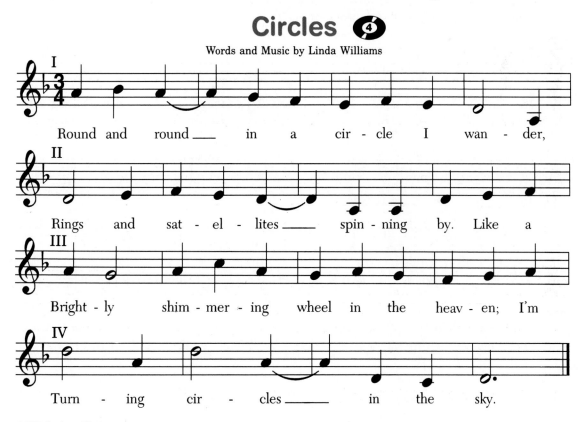

I
Round and round ___ in a cir - cle I wan - der,

II
Rings and sat - el - lites ___ spin - ning by. Like a

III
Bright - ly shim - mer - ing wheel in the heav - en; I'm

IV
Turn - ing cir - cles ___ in the sky.

67

Dots—An Uneven Rhythm

Remember the sixteenth-note pattern?

in - ter - fer - ence

Here is a different chant
for the same pattern:

dah dah dah *dee,* dah dah dah *dee*

Now, chant just the first
and last sound in each group.

dah   *dee,* dah   *dee*

There is an easier way to
write this rhythm pattern.
The dotted rhythm is found
in the song "Do, Lord."

dah - *dee,* dah - *dee*

Do, Lord

Black Spiritual

1. When chill-y winds blow from the   North, _ I've got   to   go;
2. I've   got a home in   glo-ry   land, _ out-shines   the   sun;

When chill-y winds blow from the   North, _ I've got   to   go;
I've   got a home in   glo-ry   land, _ out-shines   the   sun;

When chill-y winds blow from the   North, _ I've   got   to   go;
I've   got a home in   glo-ry   land, _ out-shines   the   sun;

REFRAIN

A - way up   be-yond _ the moon.   Do, Lord, O   do, Lord, O

68

do re-mem-ber me; Do, Lord, O do, Lord, O do re-mem-ber me;

Do, Lord, O do, Lord, O do re-mem-ber me; A-way up be-yond _ the moon.

A dotted rhythm is even featured in the countermelody and in the clapping.

Countermelody

Do, Lord, do re-mem-ber, Do, Lord, do re-mem-ber, Do re-mem-ber

me, Do re-mem-ber; Do, Lord, do re-mem-ber, do re-mem-ber me,

Way be-yond the moon.

Clap:

End with:

A Rhythmic Song

Dancing José

Words and Music by Linda Williams

1. I'll tell you a stor-y, the leg-end of Danc-ing Jo-sé. _____
sé was so ter-ri-bly shy and a-fraid he would fall. _____

I'll tell you what hap-pened in San-to Do-min-go that day. _____ A
He danced in the sha-dows up close to the old ci-ty wall. _____ But

danc-ing con-test was held in the square, And ev-'ry-one in the
then he sud-den-ly jumped in the air, And then came danc-ing out

vil-lage was there, All dressed in their best for a danc-ing fi-es-ta,
in-to the square, He whirled and he twirled in his own lit-tle world; He

1.
and there in the crowd was my old friend, Jo-sé. _____ 2. Jo-

2.,3.,4.
Refrain follows 2, 3, and 4
was Danc-ing Jo-sé, And the best of them all. _____

REFRAIN

He danced in a cir-cle all o-ver the square, A

He danced all o-ver the square, A

70

dance in   a trance as   if   no one was there, A   Two - step, a   Tan - go, a

dance   as   if   no one was there, A   fan - cy   Fan -

fan - cy   Fan - dan - go, and   *Unison:*

|2., 3.|

dan - go,   *and* Then he went danc - ing a - way._____   3.   In
                                                                   4. Now

3. (In) Santo Domingo they'll always remember his name;
    And everyone knows he went on to find fortune and fame.
    The dancing contest is held every year;
    They wait for Dancing José to appear.
    They think of the day he went dancing away,
    But he's never come back, and it isn't the same.
    Refrain:
    He danced in a circle all over the square . . .

4. (Now,) I alone know the secret of Dancing José;
    For quite by chance I was dancing beside him that day.
    When all the dancers began to compete,
    José moved back to get out of the street,
    And stepped on a cactus which made him react
    As if he'd learned to dance at the Bolshoi ballet!
    Refrain: (begin softly and get louder)
    He danced in a circle all over the square . . .

|4.| *rit.*   *unis. Slower*

way,   A - way,_____   And   that   was   the   last   that   was   seen

shout:

of Danc - ing   Jo - sé!   A - dios,   Jo - sé!   O - lé!

Melody

Sound and Pitch

Strike a piano key, pluck a guitar string, blow into a clarinet.

You have made a sound. In fact, you have made a tone with definite pitch. You can sing the tone you just played.

Now strike a drum, hit a wood block, tap two finger cymbals together. You have made a sound, but it has no definite pitch. Some of these sounds seem higher or lower than others, but you cannot sing the pitch.

Both kinds of sound—those with definite pitch and those without—can be used to make music.

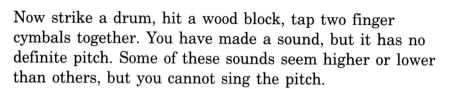

Play this familiar tune with any pitched instrument, and any set of unpitched percussion instruments. You can even invent your own percussion set from objects in your classroom.

Up and Down, By Steps and Leaps

In this song, all the pitches are next to one another. The melody moves *stepwise* upward and downward.

Annie Lee

Words and Music by Mary Hoffman

There is a val - ley, a far a - way val - ley. 'Twas there that I first saw my sweet __ An - nie Lee. Though the years have gone by, and my home's in the moun - tains, I'll nev - er for - get her, my sweet An - nie Lee.

Here is a melody that can be sung or played on the bells. Notice that the pitches do not move stepwise. The melody *leaps* from pitch to pitch.

Bells or Voices:

An - nie, An - nie, An - nie, my An - nie Lee. I'll ne - ver, ne - ver for - get her, my An - nie Lee.

You can play or sing this melody as a descant with "Annie Lee."

The Tonal Center

Cadence and Phrase

Here's a melody without a final note. Even without knowing the tune, you will probably be able to sing the last note correctly.

The note you sang can be called the *tonal center*. The rest of the melody seems to lead you to that ending. This kind of phrase ending is called a *cadence*.

A cadence is like a tonal rest stop. The melody will seem to lead to that point and rest comfortably there.

Often the cadence resting place will be at the tonal center. The note at the tonal center is the *key* note. Every scale is named for the key note at its tonal center.

A Major Scale

Here is a scale with the note *C* as its tonal center. It is in the key of C.

All of the pitches in the C scale, and in any other scale, move stepwise. They look as if they are all the same distance apart.

Let's see if this is true. Use a set of resonator bells.

Line all the bells up this way and play them in order. This is called a *chromatic scale*.

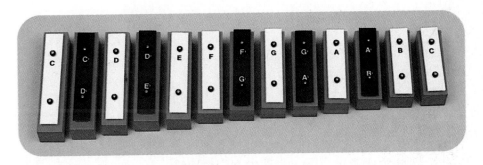

Now remove all the sharps and flats.
The scale will look like this:

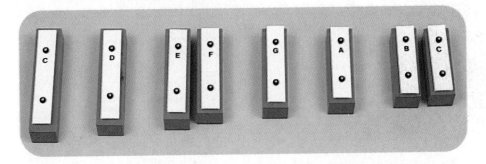

Some bells are closer together than others. The interval or space between notes 3 and 4, and between notes 7 and 8 is closer than the other intervals. This pattern—with 3 and 4, 7 and 8 occurring closer together—is the pattern of the C scale, and every other *major* scale.

"Annie Lee" is a song in a *major* key.

Minor Scales

Minor scales and minor keys sound different from major keys. They even seem to be different in mood. This happens because of changes in the way the scale is constructed.

Set up the bells as you did before. Pull out the bells for E, A, and B, leaving the E flat, A flat, and B flat.

When you play them, you will hear a new scale, the *natural minor scale*. "Dundai" is a song in a minor key.

Dundai

Hebrew Folk Song   English Words by Harold Aks

Land of Is - ra - el,   O   land   of   mine,   On

you the sun and moon and stars do shine.   Dun - dai, dun - dai, dun - dai,

Dun - dai - dai,   Dun - dai,   dun - dai, dun - dai,   Dun - dai - dai.

Hearing the Difference

Listen to this familiar round. It is in a major key.

 "Are You Sleeping"

Listen to how different it sounds as a minor tune.

Listen to these two musical fragments from the music of Bach.
The first one is in a minor key.

 Invention No. 13 . . . . .J. S. Bach

The second example is in a major key.

 Brandenburg Concerto No. 3 (excerpt)...J. S. Bach

Although both examples are played on the same instrument,
the synthesizer, and although they are in a similar style, the
difference in how they sound is partly due to one being in a
major key and the other in a minor key.

A Folk Song from Brazil

As you sing this song, listen for the changes in tonality. Does the song end in major or minor?

Tutu Maramba

Brazilian Folk Song   Words by Julia W. Bingham

Tu - tu Ma - ram - ba, stop scratch - ing at my door.

The mas - ter is home, he will fright - en you a - way.

Tu - tu Ma - ram - ba, don't come here an - y more;

My child must be safe in his sleep, in his play.

Loud - ly ring - ing bells will drive a - way all e - vil things,
Soft - ly sound the ev - 'ning bells that mark the com - ing night;

Things that lurk in dusk - y holes or dart on cru - el wings.
Na - ture sinks to peace - ful rest un - til the morn - ing light.

78

A - ran - ha Ta - tan - ha, A - ran - ha Ta - tan - ha,

If Tu - tu should come back, he must sure - ly find you sleep - ing.

A - ran - ha Ta - tan - ha, A - ran - ha Ta - tan - ha,

All night by your bed, I my watch will be keep - ing.

Pentatonic Mode

Here is a scale that uses a group of notes that are in a different pattern from the major or minor scales. There are five different pitches in this scale.

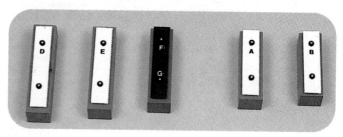

It is called a *pentatonic* scale. Here is a pentatonic song from China.

A Boat on the Lake *(Tai-hu)*

Folk Song from China   Collected by Shao-Mei Ting

Wind is blow-ing a - cross the ___ lake, Qui - et - ly ___ the
Shan ching sho - ei ming iou jing ___ jing, *hu shin peau ___ lai*
shahn cheeng sho - ay meeng yo jeeng jeeng hoo shin payau lahee

rip - ples ___ play; We row and ___ row, we row and ___ row.
feng i ___ jehn, *a shyng a ___ shyng* *a, jihn a ___ jihn,*
fung ee jehn ah sheeng ah sheeng ah jin ah jin

Few there are who walk by the shore, Where the lake ___ re -
hwang huen shyr hau ren shyng ___ shao, *baun kong yu - eh ying*
wahng wehn sheer hau rehn sheeng shau baun kawng yoo - eh yeeng

flects the ___ moon; We row and ___ row, we row and ___ row.
shoei mi - an yau, *a shyng a ___ shyng* *a, jihn a ___ jihn.*
shoay mee - ahn yau ah sheeng ah sheeng ah jin ah jin

80

Here are three bell patterns that can be used as an
ostinato for "A Boat on the Lake." Any kind of
bells that can play the five notes of this
pentatonic scale will do.

Out of the Mode

Here is a song with no mode at all. It doesn't even have a
tonal center. It uses only six pitches, from E flat to A flat.
Many modern composers like to write in a way that avoids any
mode, any tonality, any tonal center.

A Song with No Key

Words and Music by David Eddleman

How can there be a song with no key? It's hard to

see how it can be. Lis - ten to me and

rit.

you will a - gree ___ There is no key. Oh, me.

Building a Melody

Contour

Making a melody means deciding what shape it will take, what the *contour* of the tune will be. It may be very jagged, like a city skyline.

 "Gavotte" from *Classical Symphony* (excerpt) ....Prokofiev

It may move stepwise and be as smooth as rolling hills.

 "Jesu, Joy of Man's Desiring" ....Bach

Sequence

Compare these two melody patterns.

The second pattern starts on a lower pitch. This repeating of a pattern on a different pitch is called a *sequence*.

Tea for Two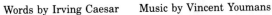

Words by Irving Caesar   Music by Vincent Youmans

Repetition and Contrast

Some songs, particularly folk songs, use repeated patterns to create a melody. Usually, however, there is a section with *contrasting* elements to make the song more interesting.

Here is a country song that is built on repeated patterns. The middle section contrasts with the rest of the song.

On the Road Again

Words and Music by Willie Nelson   Arranged by Larry Eisman

On the   road a-gain. _____   Just can't wait to get   on the
road a-gain. _____   Go-in'   pla-ces   that I've
road a-gain. _____   Just can't wait to get   on the

road a-gain. _____   The life I love is mak-ing mu-sic with my
nev-er been. _____   See-in' things that I may nev-er see a-
road a-gain. _____   The life I love is mak-ing mu-sic with my

Last time to coda

friends, and I can't wait to get on the road _ a - gain. ___ On the
gain, and I can't wait to get on the road _ a - gain. _
friends, and I can't wait to get on the road _ a - gain. ___ *Repeat entire song, then go to Coda*

On the road   a - gain, ___ Like a   band of gyp-sies   we go down the

high - way. ___ We're the best of friends, ___ In - sist - ing that the

world keep turn-ing our way, _____ and our way, _____ Is on the

I can't wait to get on the road _ a - gain. _____ And on the road _ a - gain. _____

Harmony

When you sing or play more than one tone at a time, you create *harmony*. Here is a simple melody for you to sing.

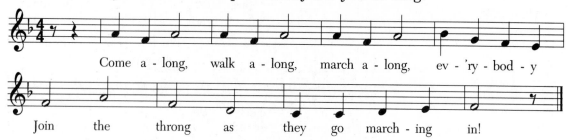

Come a - long, walk a - long, march a - long, ev - 'ry - bod - y

Join   the   throng   as   they   go   march - ing   in!

Singing in Harmony

Here is a song for you to sing in *unison,* with everyone on the same pitches:

When the Saints Go Marching In

Black Spiritual

Oh, when the saints _____ go march-ing in, _____ Oh, when the saints go march - ing in, _____ Oh, Lord, I want to be in that num - ber _____ When the saints go march - ing in.

If some students sing the melody on p. 86 while the rest sing the song, the result is harmony!

Musical Partnership

Here is a song the whole class can sing.

My Home's in Montana

American Cowboy Song   Adapted by M. Hoffman

My home's in Mon - tan - a, I wear a ban - dan - a; My

spurs are of sil - ver, my po - ny is gray. When rid - ing the

rang - es, my luck nev - er chang - es; With foot in the stir - rup I

gal - lop a - way. Home on the roll - ing range,

That's where I want to stay! When rid - ing the rang - es my

luck nev - er chang - es; With foot in the stir - rup I gal - lop a - way.

88

Here is another song of the West you can sing.

Home on the Range

American Cowboy Song

Oh, give me a home where the buf - fa - lo roam, Where the

deer and the an - te - lope play; ____ Where sel - dom is

heard a dis - cour - ag - ing word, And the skies are not cloud - y all

day. ____ Home, home on the range, ____ Where the

deer and the an - te - lope play; ____ Where sel - dom is heard a dis -

cour - ag - ing word, And the skies are not cloud - y all day. ____

Now divide the class into two sections and sing these two
songs together. You are singing in two-part harmony.

Canons

Here is a song you can sing together
and still make harmony. All you
have to do is begin at different times, as on page 91.
This kind of imitation is called a
canon.

Catch a Falling Star 5

Words and Music by Paul Vance and Lee Pockriss

Catch a fall-ing star and   put it in your pock-et,   Nev-er let it fade a -
Catch a fall-ing star and   put it in your pock-et,   Save it for a rain-y

way.   day. For   love may come and tap ____ you on the shoul-der
when your trou-bles start ____ in mul-ti-ply-ing

some star-less night.   And just in case you think ___ you want to hold her,
and they just might.   It's eas-y to for-get ___ them with-out try-ing,

you'll have a pock - et full of star-light.
with just a pock - et full of star-light. } Catch a fall-ing star and

put it in your pock-et, nev-er let it get a - way.

Catch a fall-ing star and put it in your pock-et, nev-er let it get a -

Catch a fall-ing star and put it in your pock-et, save it for a rain-y

way. Catch a fall-ing star and put it in your pock-et,

day. For Save it for a rain-y day. ____

save it for a rain-y day. For day. Save it for a rain-y day. ____

Round and Round . . .

A *round* is a kind of canon. In a round, you can sing the song
any number of times, starting over when you come to the end.
Listen to this modern round.

"A Home on the Rolling Sea" . . . . Eddleman

Harmonizing

Thirds and Sixths

Here is a song that can be harmonized in *thirds* or in *sixths*.

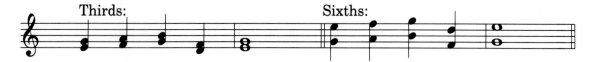

Before you sing this song, listen to the recording. The voices are singing in thirds. The instrumental section is harmonized in sixths, above the melody.

When the Chestnut Leaves Were Falling

Spanish Folk Song   English Words by Luther Wilde

1. When the chest - nut leaves were fall -
2. Then he raised his eyes to beg

ing, 'Ni - ta was tend - ing her sheep.
her, "Give me a drink if you will."

By the brook she saw a gyp - sy
'Ni - ta made a cup of rush - es

Look - ing in the wa - ter deep.____
And the gyp - sy drank his fill.____

From ON WINGS OF SONG of THE WORLD OF MUSIC series, © Copyright, 1949, 1945, by Ginn and Company. Used with permission.

You can see as well as hear the difference. The thirds in the
voice parts are closer together than the sixths in the instruments.

Listen to a song for two voices. First you will hear each voice
singing a *solo* melody. Later they will sing a *duet* in thirds.
The higher part is sung by an adult woman. The lower part is
sung by a twelve-year-old young man.

"Pie Jesu" from *Requiem* ...Andrew Lloyd Webber

Harmonizing with Chords

When several pitches sound at the same time, they create a *chord*. When you strike a combination of keys on the piano, or strum several strings at once on the guitar, you are playing a chord.

You can play chords with the resonator bells.

Make a three-note chord to play on the bells.

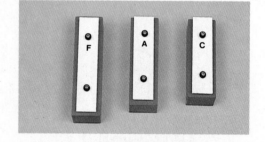

Make another chord, using different bells.

One more chord and you can play an accompaniment for "Catch a Falling Star."

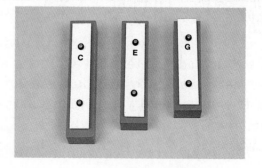

94

Chord Progressions

As you harmonize with chords, you will notice that your ear tells you when you need to change from one chord to another. This changing pattern is called the *chord progression.*

Most songs we like to sing have interesting but simple chord progressions. The most commonly used chords are the ones we make on the first, fourth, and fifth notes in the scale.

In the key of D those three chords look like this:

Most of the songs in your book have letter names above the melody.

Using the chords illustrated at the top of the page, add an instrument and harmonize with the chords. Play an accompaniment for the partner songs on p. 88.

Form—A Musical Blueprint

No one can build a house just by drawing a picture of it and labeling the sections.

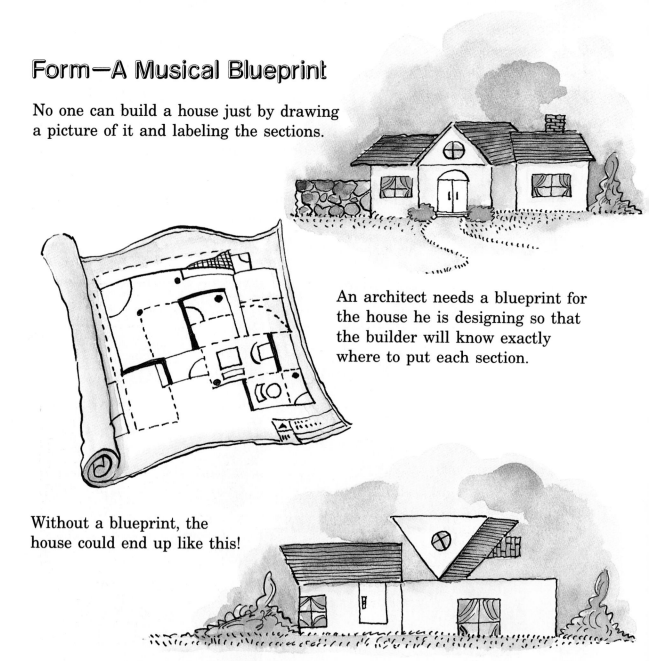

An architect needs a blueprint for the house he is designing so that the builder will know exactly where to put each section.

Without a blueprint, the house could end up like this!

Composers, like architects, have a plan for their compositions. Musical ideas and events cannot be put together in just any way. Try this version of a familiar song.

See how they run! Three blind mice. They all ran af-ter the farm-er's wife, See how they run! They all ran af-ter the farm-er's wife,

Music Taking Shape

A pile of bricks takes shape in the hands of an expert bricklayer. In the same way, musical ideas take shape in the hands of a composer or songwriter.

In music, contrasting sections are extremely important. If a piece of music were the same from beginning to end, we would soon grow tired of it.

Listen to this piece played by Dave Brubeck.

 "Take Five" (excerpt) .... Desmond

You have learned to call this form ABA.

"Dundai" on p. 76 also has an A and a B section. However, the A does not return. The form is AB.

Mix and Match

You can play an ABA percussion piece, using maracas and a guiro.

Here is the A section, played on maracas:

Shake:

The B section is played by scraping the guiro.

Scrape:

Clap this pattern while two solo players use the A and B patterns to create an ABA percussion piece.

Clap:

You can use your ABA percussion pattern to accompany the song on p. 99. The form is the same.

Perform it this way: (Continue the basic clapping beat throughout.) Play A twice, B once, then return to A, this time playing it only once.

No-Name Bossa Nova 5

Words and Music by Mary E. Hoffman

Do the No-Name Bos-sa No - va, ___ Do the No-Name Bos-sa No - va. ___

We were danc - ing ___ in the ___ sha - dows ___ While a ___
danc - ing ___ in the ___ sha - dows ___ But we ___

qui - et ___ La - tin gui - tar strummed us ___ a new tune, ___ a
have - n't ___ thought of a name to give to ___ that new tune, ___ the

new tune ___ that had no name, Do the No-Name Bos-sa No - va, ___
new tune ___ that has no name,

Do the No-Name Bos-sa No - va. ___ We ___ swayed to the rhy - thm ___

___ De - signed ___ for tro - pi - cal nights. ___ This ___ me - lo - dy

B MIN₇ E₇ A₇ D₇ C#₉ Eb₉

haunts us ___ It ech - oes with such de - lights ___ We're still ___

Coda

Do the No-Name Bos-sa No - va. ___

Forming a Rondo

Here are lines from three songs in our book. Sing them in order.

A E - ze - kiel__ saw the wheel, Way up in the mid-dle of the air.

B Swing low, sweet char - i - ot___ Com - in' for to car - ry me home.

C Now let me fly, _____ Now let me fly, _____ Now
let me fly__ in - to Mount Zi - on, Lord, Lord. _____

Now mix them up any way you want to. The three musical
elements work in almost any order, except that one of them
sounds unfinished. Try it this way:

Sing:  (A) [B] (A) △C (A)

We have turned these bits of songs into a vocal *rondo*.

A rondo keeps coming around to a main musical idea, in this
case the melody we chose to be *A*.

Rondo form his been popular for several centuries. It is a good
way to have interesting contrasting sections and still have a
familiar idea to return to. Listen to this rondo.

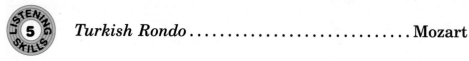

5 LISTENING SKILLS *Turkish Rondo* . . . . **Mozart**

100

Variations

Another kind of form is *Theme and Variations*.

Themes, or musical ideas, are varied in a number of ways. Composers can be very clever in the way they write variations. Often a composer chooses a familiar tune for a set of variations.

The theme can be played slower or faster, and with changed rhythm patterns. The theme can be turned upside down, or can be decorated with extra notes to make it fancier.

Here is a famous set of variations written by Charles Ives. As you listen to the recording, you will recognize the theme. In fact, you will be able to hear the theme in each variation. However, the personality of the melody has been changed completely in each variation.

Variations on "America" (excerpt) . . . . Ives

Charles Ives
(1874–1954)

American composer Charles Ives lived all his life in New England. He was a prosperous insurance company executive who wrote music in his spare time.

His music was very experimental for his time. It was not appreciated by the public until he was quite old and no longer composing. In 1947, when Ives was in his 70s and no longer writing music, he was awarded a Pulitzer Prize for his Third Symphony.

Style

Some pieces of music, particularly songs, are timeless. They seem to speak to every age.

Just such a song is "Scarborough Fair." It is an old English folk song with origins that go back many centuries. It has come down to us in several versions. This is one of the most popular.

Scarborough Fair

English Folk Song

1. Are you go - ing to Scar - bor - ough Fair?
2. Tell her to make me a cam - bric shirt,   Pars - ley, sage, rose - mar - y and thyme;
3. Tell her to wash it in yon - der well,

Re - mem - ber me to one who lives there —
With - out a seam or nee - dle work —   She once was a true love of mine.
Where nev - er rain or wa - ter fell —

Folk songs like this one are part of our heritage.

However, musical styles change from age to age. A musician can recognize, through musical clues, the time a certain piece of music was written.

Musical Time Travel

Let us take our song "Scarborough Fair" through a time trip from the Middle Ages to the present day. We will hear it as it might have been used in different time periods.

6 LISTENING SKILLS — "Scarborough Fair" Variation 1

6 LISTENING SKILLS — "Scarborough Fair" Variation 2

6 LISTENING SKILLS — "Scarborough Fair" Variation 3

More Time Travel . . .

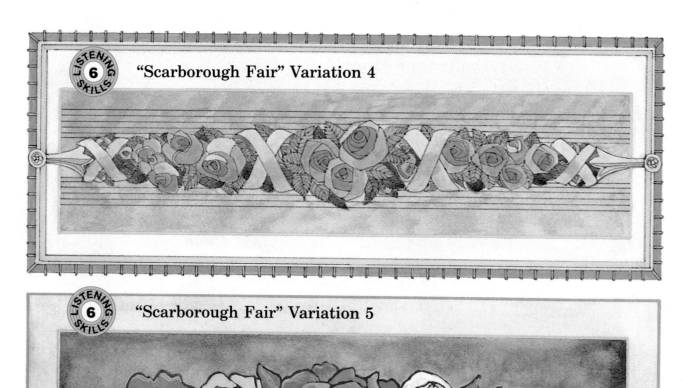

6 "Scarborough Fair" Variation 4

6 "Scarborough Fair" Variation 5

6 "Scarborough Fair" Variation 6

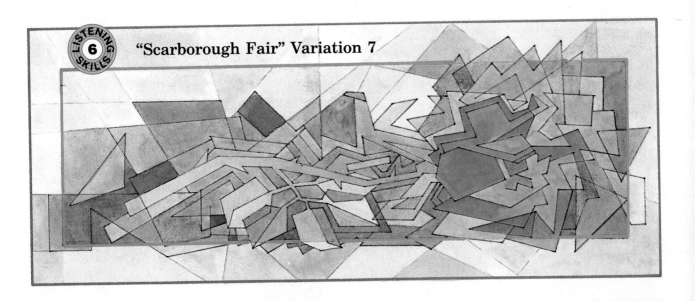

Call Chart 4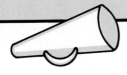

Listen for the musical clues that will tell you the historical period for each of these musical excerpts. You should be able to identify the period by the style of the music.

6 *Styles Montage:*

1. *Gregorian Chant* ....Anonymous

2. *Gigue* ....Byrd

3. *Gavotte* ....Bach

4. *Sonata in C Major* ....Mozart

5. *Piano Concerto No. 2*................Rachmaninoff

6. "Festivals" from *Nocturnes*................Debussy

7. "Sacrificial Dance" from *Rite of Spring*..Stravinsky

Musical Interaction

Musical *interaction* is like a musical conversation. It can sound like questions and answers, a lively debate, or even a friendly musical argument.

This pattern of musical interaction is known as "call and response."

Long John 6

Blues Song

With his shin-y blade, _ *With his shin-y blade,* _ Got it in his hand, _ *Got it in his hand,* _ Gon-na chop out the live oaks, *Gon-na chop out the live oaks,* That are in this land, _ *That are in this land.* _ He's Long John, _ *He's Long John,* _ He's long gone, _ *He's long gone,* _ He's gone, gone, __ *He's gone, gone,* __ Like a

tur - key in the corn, _ Like a tur - key in the corn, _ With his

long clothes on, _ With his long clothes on, _ He's long gone, _ He's long gone, _ He's

long gone, _ He's long gone, _ He's gone, He's long gone. _

A Diagram for Musical Interaction

Sometimes an instrument or voice sounds alone. Listen to this violin piece by Bach.

 "Presto" from *Sonata in G Minor for Unaccompanied Violin* (excerpt)........J. S. Bach

Use the symbol ◇ for one instrument or voice sounding alone.

More often, a number of instruments or voices will perform together. Listen to this string "Serenade" by Mozart.

 "Minuet" from *Eine Kleine Nachtmusik* (excerpt) ..
...................................W. A. Mozart

Use the symbol ◇◇◇ for a group of instruments or voices.

In "Long John" the solo voice and the chorus take turns.

The recording of "Long John" includes an *accompaniment*.

Another Pattern for Call and Response

In "Long John" the call and response were exactly alike. The chorus simply echoed what they heard in the solo voice.

Often, however, the response will be different. In "Michael, Row the Boat Ashore," the group response of "Hallelujah" is different from the solo call.

Michael, Row the Boat Ashore

Black American Work Song

On the recording of "Michael, Row the Boat Ashore," the solo voice and group chorus are accompanied by a solo piano.

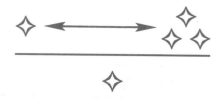

108

A Call and Response for Instruments

Listen to a piece for solo trumpet and string instruments.

 Sonata for Trumpet and Strings,
Movement 1 . . . . Henry Purcell

You can hear the musical interaction. The pattern is very similar to one of the call and response songs. Which one is it most like?

or

The pattern of this chant is also like one of the call and response songs. Which one is it most like?

Train Chant 6

Jean Riddle

Solo: All a - board for In - di - an - a!
etc. *(Make up new verses)*

Chorus: All a - board! All a - board!

Sandblocks:

All a - board for Ten - nes - see!

Ev - 'ry - bo - dy, all a - board!

Sounds Against Sounds—Antiphonal Music

Composers sometimes use one set of sounds alternating with another set of sounds. This is called *antiphonal* music.

You have probably already guessed that call and response is one kind of antiphonal music. Another kind of antiphonal pattern can be called "group alternating with group."

Listen to this piece by George Frideric Handel. It is an antiphonal piece for instruments, with three sets of instruments trading off. Sometimes one group will sound by itself, and sometimes two will sound at the same time. Once in a while they all play together.

 "Allegro" from *Water Music*...........G. F. Handel

Following a Score

If you listen to a piece of music while you follow the printed score, you can *see* the musical interaction as well as hear it.

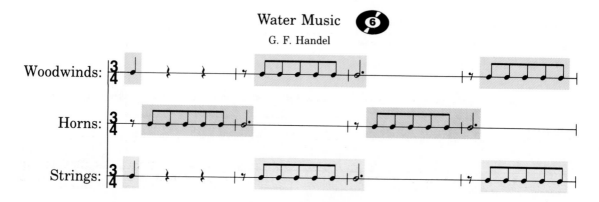

Water Music
G. F. Handel

111

Antiphonal Music for Voices

An ancient "Echo Song" by Orlando di Lasso uses two groups of voices.

The first group sings, followed by the second group singing exactly the same phrase. The two groups overlap a little, and the *antiphonal* effect is like a real echo.

 "Echo Song" .... Orlando di Lasso

Make your own "echo."

Echoes

Bell or Voices:

I — Fol-low, fol-low me, Oh, fol-low me, Oh, fol-low me.

II — Fol-low, fol-low me, Oh, fol-low me, Oh, fol-low me.

The Magic of Repeated Patterns

As the elements of a piece of music interact, our ears often notice *repetition* before anything else.

Even works of visual art sometimes use repeated patterns to catch our attention. This kind of pattern is almost like a "visual echo."

Listen to this example and see if you find a resemblance between the music and the pictures on these pages.

AMRAGA *(Morning Raga)* . . . . James Roberts

A Musical S.O.S.

The rock singer and composer Sting often closes his live concerts with this song. Notice how repetition gives a special power to the message of the song.

Message in a Bottle

Words and Music by Sting

1. Just a cast - a - way __ an is - land lost __ at sea __
2. A __ year __ has passed __ since I wrote my note, __

__ o, __ An - oth - er lone - ly day, __
I should have known __ it right __ from the

No one here __ but me, __ o, __ More
start; On - ly hope __

lone - li - ness __ than an - y - one __ could bear, __
__ can keep __ me to - geth - er __

Res - cue me __ be - fore __ I fall __ in - to __ des - pair, __
Love __ can mend __ your life, __ but love __ can break __ your heart. __

The Artist's Medium

When artists choose a subject they want to express visually, they must choose the *medium* in which to work.

An artist may choose, for example, oil paint as the best medium for a particular work of art. Another artist may decide to interpret that same subject in stone.

Each artist has chosen the medium that best expresses a particular feeling and response to the subject.

The Composer's Medium

A composer must choose a *musical medium* to express a musical idea. This is only one of the many decisions a composer must make, but it is a very important one.

In music, the medium is the choice of instruments, voices, or combinations that will be used to make the sounds of music.

Listen to this piece by the French composer Maurice Ravel. The composer made two different choices: he wrote it first for piano.

"Minuet" from *Le Tombeau de Couperin* . . . . . Ravel

1. Piano solo (excerpt)

2. Symphony orchestra (excerpt)

Maurice Ravel
(1875–1937)

French composer Maurice Ravel lived most of his life in this century. He wrote many famous piano pieces, but is best known for his orchestral piece, "Bolero."

Ravel often wrote a piece for piano, and then rewrote the same piece for orchestra, as he did with the "Minuet."

Ravel was considered one of the most skillful orchestrators of his time. His pieces are full of beautiful orchestral "color." His style has often been copied by writers of television and movie music.

He admired American composer George Gershwin so much that he used a jazz style on one of his piano concertos.

The Artist's Palette

An artist uses visual colors, choosing the ones that will help express an idea or feeling about the subject of a painting.

Vibrant, warm reds and oranges? Cool, liquid blues and greens? Shimmering yellows and golds?

Rouen Cathedral (Harmony in Blue)
by Claude Monet.

Rouen Cathedral (West facade — Sunlight)
by Claude Monet.

The colors in a painting may be quiet and subdued or bright and bold. It all depends on the choices the artist makes in order to express visual ideas.

The Composer's Palette

The composer's "palette" is as varied and colorful as the painter's. Composers use *tone color* to express musical ideas.

Listen to these two short musical sketches. Think of them as musical pictures, or as abstract, colorful designs. One is dark and somber and one is bright and cheerful.

 "Bydlo" from *Pictures at an Exhibition* (excerpt) .. . . .Mussorgsky

 Overture from *Candide* (excerpt) . . . . Bernstein

A painter may use contrasting colors or may highlight sections of a painting to make the work more interesting.

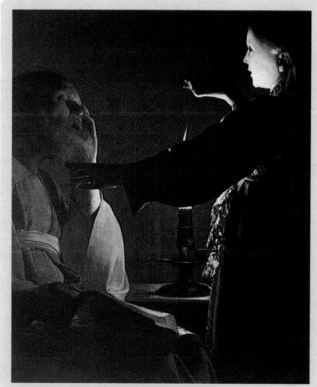

Angel appearing to St. Joseph asleep
Georges de la Tour

A composer may do the same thing with sound. Listen to the way a great composer used the bright tone color of the piccolo to add "shine" to the ending of a symphony.

 Symphony No. 5 "Finale" (excerpt) . . . . . . Beethoven

A Colorful Song for Young Musicians

Here is a song about the tone colors of several instruments.
Each is introduced individually, with a lot of bragging.
Eventually they all become a colorful "orchestra."

I Am a Great Musician

Traditional   Melodic Adaptation and New Words by Linda Williams

1. I am a great mu-si-cian, I prac-tice ev-'ry day,
   And peo-ple come from miles a-round   Just to hear me play
2. I am a great mu-si-cian, that's what I hear them say.
   They come and set up fold-ing chairs   just to hear me play

My trum-pet, my trum-pet, I love to play my trum-pet:
My vi-o-lin, my vi-o-lin, I love to play my vi-o-lin:

*Solo 1 (trumpet)

Ta-ra-ta-ra, Ta-ra-ta-ra, Ta-ra, Ta-ra-ra, Ta-ra!

Solo 2 (violin)

La la la la la la la la la la la la la la.

Solo 3 (clarinet)

Doo-dle-dee doo-dle, Doo-dle-dee doo-dle, Doo-dle-dee doo-dle-dee doo.

120

Solo 4 (string bass)

Thum   thum   thum   thum   thum   thum   thum.

Solo 5 (piccolo)

Dee-dle dee-dee-dee, Dee-dle dee-dee-dee,   Dee-dle dee-dle dee dee dee-dle dee.

*(Each soloist sings the "instrument" part,
and is joined, on the repeat, by all the
others who have already been introduced.)

3. I am a great musician, and just the other day
   A hundred people stood in line just to hear me play
   My clarinet . . .

4. I am a great musician, and people have to pay
   To get a perfect front row seat just to hear me play
   My string bass . . .

5. I am a great musician, I'm not ashamed to say
   The paper sent reporters out just to hear me play
   My piccolo . . .

6. (Slower) All:
   We'll all be great musicians, we'll practice every day,
   We hope you'll come from miles around
   Just to hear us play, (to Coda)

Coda   a tempo

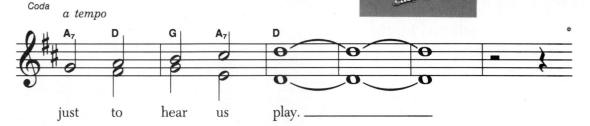

just   to   hear   us   play. _____

*Each "musician" sings the instrumental line to finish the song.

The Colors of the Orchestra

Painting With Sound

A composer paints pictures and designs with musical sound. The particular sound each instrument makes is called *tone color*.
Tone color is affected by the materials of the instrument.

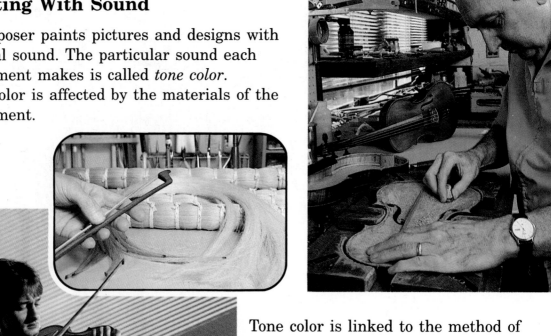

Tone color is linked to the method of sound production, whether a sound is made by scraping, blowing, striking, or in some other way.

Tone color is affected by the size and shape of the instrument.

Listen to the opening of this piece by Berlioz, and notice the colorful use of the instruments.

 Roman Carnival Overture (excerpt)........Berlioz

Hector Berlioz
(1803–1869)

Hector Berlioz was a famous composer when he was still quite young. He had a very colorful personality, and often did things that shocked a lot of people. He was a little like some of our rock stars!

He wrote many famous works, including the *Symphony Fantastique,* which is one of the most popular symphony pieces, even today.

Berlioz was very good at choosing and using the colors of the orchestra. He is often spoken of as a musical "colorist." Many of the special effects he created were far ahead of his time.

Woodwinds

Piccolo

Flute

Oboe

English horn

Clarinet

Bassoon

Horn

Trumpet

Trombone

Tuba

Timpani

Percussion

Violins I

Violins II

Viola

Cello

Bass

A symphony orchestra contains the instrumental colors a composer needs to paint his musical pictures. The conductor knows which instruments will be playing by looking at a *score*. You can see which instruments the composer has asked for in this piece by looking at the piece of the score printed on the margin of the page.

The woodwind instruments are first in order at the top of the score.

The woodwind instruments with the highest-pitched sounds are the flute and piccolo.

The piccolo is very similar to the flute, but it is smaller and has a higher, more piercing sound.

 Lieutenant Kije (excerpt: piccolo) . . . . Prokofiev

The flute has a high, sweet sound.

 Daphnis and Chloe (excerpt: flute) . . . . Ravel

Next in order on the score are the oboe, then the English horn.

The oboe has an exotic, edgy sound.

 Polovetsian Dance (excerpt: oboe) . . . . Borodin

The English horn sound is similar, but darker and deeper.

 Roman Carnival Overture (excerpt: English horn). .
. . . . Berlioz

The next instrument on the score is the clarinet, followed by the bassoon.

The clarinet has a clear, mellow sound.

 Peter and the Wolf (excerpt: clarinet) .... Prokofiev

The reedy voice of the bassoon is the lowest-pitched of the woodwind instruments.

 Sorcerer's Apprentice (excerpt: bassoon) ....Dukas

 Woodwind Fantasy on a Thanksgiving Song ....B. Red

Brass

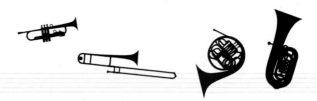

Piccolo

Flute

Oboe

English horn

Clarinet

Bassoon

Horn

Trumpet

Trombone

Tuba

Timpani

Percussion

I
Violins
II

Viola

Cello

Bass

The bright-sounding brass instruments come next.

The mellow, rather "fuzzy" sound of the French horns goes well with either the brass instruments or the woodwinds.

 Till Eulenspiegel's Merry Pranks (excerpt: horn)...
....Strauss

The trumpet has a number of sounds and styles that it can play. It is very effective in fanfares and marches. Listen to this familiar march from an opera.

 "Grand March" from *Aida* (excerpt: trumpets)...................................Verdi

Joshua's Capture of Jericho
Jean Fouquet

The horn and trumpet both have coiled tubing. Otherwise they would take up too much space. An ancient kind of trumpet with straight tubing is sometimes used for special occasions. It is used to make an announcement or to introduce someone very important.

Low Brass

Piccolo

Flute

Oboe

English horn

Clarinet

Bassoon

Horn

Trumpet

Trombone

Tuba

Timpani

Percussion

I
Violins

II

Viola

Cello

Bass

The trombone is the only instrument that changes pitch with the use of a *slide*. The trombone can sound very quiet and sweet, but it can also play very loud sounds.

 "Pilgrim's Chorus" from *Tannhauser* (excerpt: trombones) .... Wagner

The tuba has a low, dark sound.

 Pictures at an Exhibition "Bydlo" (excerpt) .... Mussorgsky

Listen to the sound of the brass instruments playing together as a *brass choir* in the accompaniment for this song.

God of Our Fathers ⑦

Words by Daniel C. Roberts   Music by George W. Warren

Majestically

1. God of our fa - thers, whose al - might - y hand
2. Thy love di - vine hath led us in the past,
3. Re - fresh thy peo - ple on their toil - some way,

Leads forth in beau - ty all the star - ry band
In this free land by thee our lot is cast;
Lead us from night to nev - er - end - ing day;

Of shin - ing worlds in splen - dor through the skies,
Be thou our rul - er, guard - ian, guide, and stay,
Fill all our lives with love and grace di - vine,

Our grate - ful songs be - fore thy throne a - rise.
Thy word our law, thy paths our cho - sen way.
And glo - ry, laud, and praise be ev - er thine.

Brass instruments have loud, assertive voices. However, they can also play softly and can sound very lyrical when the music calls for it.

Percussion

The percussion section adds excitement and color to the sound of the orchestra. Percussion instruments are most often used to emphasize the rhythm of a piece of music.

 Symphony No. 9 (excerpt: percussion)...Beethoven

However, percussion sounds are sometimes used to create special effects, sometimes without playing any beat at all.

 Sundance (excerpt: percussion)..........Williams

Percussion instruments are generally divided into two groups: those that play definite pitches, and those that play sounds with no definite pitch.

Snare drum and bass drum are instruments of indefinite pitch. They usually play strong rhythm patterns. The cymbals add splashes of sound.

 *Battery* (excerpt: snare drum, bass drum, cymbals) ....Williams

Percussion instruments of definite pitch include the *mallet instruments*. The xylophone, orchestra bells, marimba, and chimes are all mallet instruments, and can play melodies.

Listen to the sound of the xylophone. The composer wanted to use an instrument that could sound like "old bones."

 "Fossils" from *Carnival of the Animals* (excerpt: xylophone)...................Saint-Säens

The chimes are often used to sound like church bells or clocks.

 "Great Gate at Kiev" from *Pictures at an Exhibition* (excerpt: chimes)...........Mussorgsky

The orchestra bells, marimba, and other mallet instruments are often used to add an edge to a melody line played by another instrument. Although they can be used to play tunes, they are often used to create interesting colors or textures.

The timpani, sometimes called kettledrums, can play definite pitches. Listen for the timpani in this short excerpt:

 "Sherzo" from *Symphony No. 9* (excerpt: timpani)................................Beethoven

Strings

Piccolo

Flute

Oboe

English horn

Clarinet

Bassoon

Horn

Trumpet

Trombone

Tuba

Timpani

Percussion

I
Violins
II

Viola

Cello

Bass

The orchestral string instruments are the violin, viola, cello, and string bass. The string section forms the main body of any symphony orchestra.

The violin is the highest sounding orchestral string instrument, followed by the viola, cello, and string bass. There are some notes that are the same on the violin, viola, and cello.

Listen to the way the strings sound when they are all playing on the same pitches.

LISTENING SKILLS 7 "Jupiter" from *The Planets* (excerpt: string section)...................................Holst

Violins have a wide range and can play very high.

LISTENING SKILLS 7 *Young Person's Guide to the Orchestra* (excerpt: violins) ....Britten

The viola is a larger version of the violin. Its sound is dark and mellow.

 Concerto No. 2 (excerpt: violas) ...... Rachmaninoff

The low-voiced cello has a rich, mellow sound.

 Symphony No. 5 (excerpt: cellos)...... Tchaikovsky

The string bass has a very deep voice.

 Lieutenant Kije Suite (excerpt:
    string bass) .... Prokofiev

String instruments make a warm, singing sound when playing together. The recording of this song is accompanied by a string group.

Alleluia

Music by W. A. Mozart   Adapted by Joseph Fisch

*When each voice reaches this measure, the next voice begins
line one. Each voice sings the canon twice through, then stops. This
way the canon ends with a single voice.

Putting It All Together

These young musicians are playing in a regional youth symphony. Many of them will go on to careers in music. They play the same instruments and the same music as an adult symphony orchestra.

Roman Carnival Overture (excerpt: full orchestra) . . . . Berlioz

Norwalk Youth Symphony (Connecticut)   Conducted by Gisele Ben-Dor

Careers in Music

Making a Career as a Violin Soloist

A performer whose ability and dexterity are far above the usual level is sometimes called a *virtuoso*.

Listen to part of a virtuoso piece played by a young violinist named Gil Shaham. You will be able to tell that he is a performer of great skill. He is also able to perform very expressively. The ability to create a mood and to express emotion in music is just as important as technical skill.

Carmen Fantasy (excerpt)........
.................Bizet/Sarasate

Listen to what he has to say about becoming a virtuoso violinist.

 8 **Interview with Gil Shaham**

Here Comes the Band!

What is a band? How is it different from an orchestra? Where might you hear a band? Where did bands originate?

The music a band plays can be sweet and mellow, but it is often very loud, exciting, and rhythmic. Here is a band song to sing. It describes the excitement of watching a marching band at a Saint Patrick's Day celebration.

MacNamara's Band ⑧

Words by John J. Stanford   Music by Shamus O'Connor

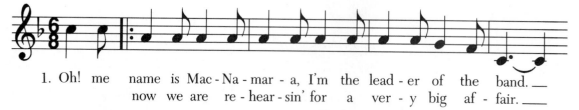

1. Oh! me name is Mac-Na-mar-a, I'm the lead-er of the band. __
now we are re-hear-sin' for a ver-y big af-fair. __

Al-though we're few in num-bers we're the fin-est in the land.
The an-nual cel-e-bra-tion, all the gen-try will be there.

We play at wakes and wed-dings and at ev-'ry fan-cy ball, ___
When Gene-ral Grant to Ire-land came he took me by the hand, ___

And when we play at fun-er-als we play the march from Saul.
Says he, "I nev-er saw the likes of Mac-Na-mar-a's band."

Oh! the drums go bang, and the cym-bals clang, and the horns they blaze a-way; ___

Mc-Car-thy pumps the old bas-soon while I the pipes do play; And,

Hen-nes-sey Ten-nes-see toot-les the flute, and the mus-ic is some-thin' grand; ___

Fine

A cred-it to old I-re-land is Mac-Na-mar-a's band.

15 1. 2. *D.S. al Fine*

2. Right Oh! the

Usually the term *band* means a group of musicians who play
wind and percussion instruments—from a few up to
hundreds—including brasses, woodwinds, and various drums,
cymbals, and other noisemakers.

An Ancient Tradition

Bands have existed for thousands of years. There were bands even before there was a system for writing down music. References to bands are found in the Bible. Probably these were trumpets and drums used for military ceremonies and for signals during battle.

During the Middle Ages and Renaissance in Europe, each town had a band. These town bands probably played for community events as well as for military parades. Gradually, over the years, the number of players in a band increased.

Ceremonies and Celebrations

Through the ages, the sounds of wind and percussion instruments have signaled important events and ceremonies. *Fanfares*—bright-sounding trumpet calls—have been played to introduce important people or proclamations.

 "Overture" to *La Peri* (excerpt) . . . . Dukas

Band music is still played on special occasions in military or political settings. One of the most exciting things about a parade is the sound of a marching band.

Even in concert, a band can make a stirring, exciting sound rarely found in other kinds of music. One of the most famous American band composers was John Philip Sousa. His marches have become concert and parade favorites all over the world.

 Semper Fidelis . . . . Sousa

Band Music for Dancing

Bands have always been ideal for playing dance music. Wind and percussion instruments can play loudly and rhythmically. The band music can be heard over the noise of people laughing and talking as they slide, jump, and stamp around a dance floor.

American dance bands have taken many forms over the years, but they have always been popular.

A Song for Waltzing

Here is a song that was very popular in 1895. The melody is in 3/4 time, so the dance that Casey and his "strawberry blonde" were doing was the *waltz*.

The Band Played On

Words by John E. Palmer   Music by Charles B. Ward

Guitar:

Ca - sey would waltz with a straw - ber - ry blonde, And the band played on. He'd glide 'cross the floor with the girl he a - dor'd and the band played on. But his brain was so load - ed it near - ly ex - plod - ed. The poor girl would shake with a - larm. He'd ne'er leave the girl with the straw - ber - ry curl, And the band played on.

School Bands in America

Think of a school subject that can begin in grade school and continue through high school and even college, one where you might sit down, or stand, or march. You might even wear a uniform, and you would always have to do everything in time.

That subject would be band. If your school has a band, it is part of a strong American tradition.

Come Hear the Band

Words and Music by David Eddleman and Linda Williams

Hear the Band

A kind of band often found in schools is the *concert band.* Band members often form other kinds of ensembles. They may put on uniforms and become a *marching band* for parades and sports events. They may form a *stage band,* using instruments from the Swing era bands of the 1930s and 40s. A stage band might perform jazz and rock pieces, or arrangements from the swing era, like this popular piece from the 1940s.

"A String of Pearls" .... Gray

A Famous Band Composer

Many famous composers have written pieces for concert band. Here is a concert band piece to listen to. You will probably recognize one of the themes.

"Fantasia on Dargason" from *Suite for Band* .... Gustav Holst

Gustav Holst
(1875–1935)

Gustav Holst was an English composer whose music was often inspired by oriental subjects or English folklore. His best-known work, a piece for orchestra called *The Planets,* is based on the eight planets of the solar system that were known in his time.

Holst was a very important teacher of music. He might have written more, but his health was poor and working at composing was often very difficult for him.

Holst's two band suites are among the best and most important works for concert band.

8 *Rhythm Patterns*

You will hear ten melodies. The rhythm pattern of each example is repeated several times. Each number is followed by two written rhythm patterns. Circle the rhythm pattern you hear.

1.

2.

3.

4.

5.

6.

7.

8.

9.

10.

Test 3

Here are eight examples of *tied* notes. After each tied-note example you will find two choices of notes that equal the time value of the tied notes. Circle the correct note. The first example has been done for you.

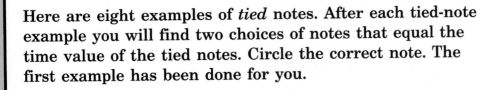

1. 𝅗𝅥 ‿ 𝅘𝅥 = 𝅝   (𝅗𝅥.)

2. 𝅗𝅥 ‿ 𝅘𝅥 = 𝅗𝅥   𝅗𝅥.

3. 𝅗𝅥 ‿ 𝅘𝅥𝅮 = 𝅗𝅥.   𝅗𝅥

4. 𝅗𝅥 ‿ 𝅗𝅥 = 𝅗𝅥.   𝅝

5. 𝅘𝅥𝅮 ‿ 𝅘𝅥𝅮 = 𝅘𝅥.   𝅘𝅥

6. 𝅘𝅥𝅮 ‿ 𝅘𝅥 = 𝅘𝅥.   𝅗𝅥

7. 𝅗𝅥 ‿ 𝅗𝅥 = 𝅗𝅥.   𝅝

8. 𝅘𝅥𝅮 ‿ 𝅘𝅥𝅯 = 𝅘𝅥   𝅘𝅥𝅮.

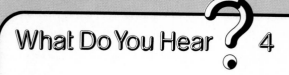
  Major and Minor Tonalities

You will hear ten instrumental examples. They are accompaniments for songs in your book. Some are in *major* keys and some in *minor*. Circle the tonality you hear in each example, major or minor.

1.   MAJOR   MINOR

2.   MAJOR   MINOR

3.   MAJOR   MINOR

4.   MAJOR   MINOR

5.   MAJOR   MINOR

6.   MAJOR   MINOR

7.   MAJOR   MINOR

8.   MAJOR   MINOR

9.   MAJOR   MINOR

10.   MAJOR   MINOR

Test 4

Here are ten melodies. Each has a very different melodic
contour or shape. Some of the melodies move mostly *by
step.* Some move mostly *by leap.* Look at each one. Write **S**
in the space if the melody moves mostly by **step.** Write **L** if
the melody moves mostly by **leap.**

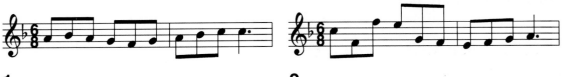

1. _____   2. _____

3. _____   4. _____

5. _____   6. _____

7. _____   8. _____

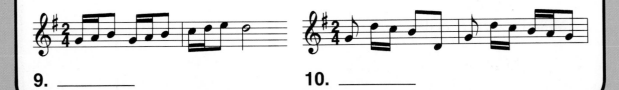

9. _____   10. _____

What Do You Hear ? 5

Harmony Patterns

You will hear six songs from your book. Each is sung in *harmony*. After each number, write the letter that tells how the harmony is made.

1. _____

2. _____

3. _____

4. _____

5. _____

6. _____

A. Harmony in thirds

B. Melody with countermelody

C. Partner songs

D. Canon

E. Melody with ostinato

F. Melody with chords

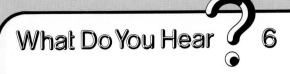

What Do You Hear 6

Form

You will hear seven musical examples. Each example will be in one of three forms: Some will have only one musical idea, and will use it in variations. Some will have two musical ideas and alternate them in an A B A form. Some will have two ideas, but will appear in an A B form.

After each example, circle the correct form.

1. Variations   A B A   A B

2. Variations   A B A   A B

3. Variations   A B A   A B

4. Variations   A B A   A B

5. Variations   A B A   A B

6. Variations   A B A   A B

7. Variations   A B A   A B

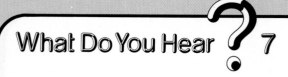

What Do You Hear 7

 Musical Interaction

You will hear seven musical examples. You will listen for
the *musical interaction*. Use the diagrams to indicate
which kind of musical interaction you hear.

◇ ⟵⟶ ◇◇◇ = solo alternating with group

◇◇◇ ⟵⟶ ◇◇◇ = group alternating with group

Circle the correct diagram for each example.

1. ◇ ⟵⟶ ◇◇◇   ◇◇◇ ⟵⟶ ◇◇◇

2. ◇ ⟵⟶ ◇◇◇   ◇◇◇ ⟵⟶ ◇◇◇

3. ◇ ⟵⟶ ◇◇◇   ◇◇◇ ⟵⟶ ◇◇◇

4. ◇ ⟵⟶ ◇◇◇   ◇◇◇ ⟵⟶ ◇◇◇

5. ◇ ⟵⟶ ◇◇◇   ◇◇◇ ⟵⟶ ◇◇◇

6. ◇ ⟵⟶ ◇◇◇   ◇◇◇ ⟵⟶ ◇◇◇

7. ◇ ⟵⟶ ◇◇◇   ◇◇◇ ⟵⟶ ◇◇◇

What Do You Hear 8

Tone Color

You will hear eight short musical examples. Listen for the tone colors in order to identify the instruments you hear. Circle the correct instrument or combination of instruments for each number. The first example has been done for you.

1.   Concert band   Full orchestra

2.   Trumpet and strings   Oboe and orchestra

3.   Brass instruments   Woodwind instruments

4.   Solo violin   Solo clarinet

5.   Brass instruments   Woodwind instruments

6.   Piano and orchestra   Percussion ensemble

7.   Drums and cymbals   Xylophone and strings

8.   Trumpet and orchestra String ensemble

SHARING MUSIC

Using Your Voice

Take a Big Breath

Before you can speak or sing, you first have to breathe. The breath you take is very important when you are singing.

If you breathe correctly, you can expand your lungs to hold a greater volume of air. This will make it easier to sing. You can sing longer without taking a breath, and you will have more air to help you control your singing.

When you are quietly breathing, the air is released through your mouth or nose with very little sound. When you want to sing or speak, you let the air vibrate a set of vocal cords, or folds deep in your throat. This is the way the sound is created.

The higher we want to sing or speak, the faster the cords must vibrate. We are so used to the way we change the pitch of our voices that we do not have to think about how we do it. It simply seems to happen.

However, we can control the sound, the pitch and loudness, even the tone quality of our voices. And we use our breath to control all of these changes.

Making Musical Phrases

Sing this song, taking a breath only
at the end of each phrase line. Notice
that some phrases are longer than others.
You will need more breath for these longer
phrases.

Bye-Bye, Blues

Words and Music by Fred Hamm, Dave Bennett, Bert Lown, and Chauncey Gray

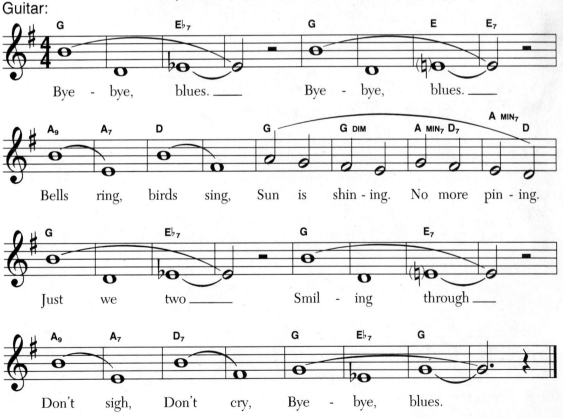

Sing It—Clearly!

Here is a song that tells a story. There are three verses with a refrain in between each verse and at the end. As you and your classmates sing the song, imagine that you are singing the story to an audience. Pronounce the words clearly and as nearly together as you can, so a listener can follow the story.

As you perform "Dona Dona," you will find the *accelerando* section at the end will be the most difficult part of this song. *Accelerando* means "getting faster and faster," and you will have to listen carefully to one another to stay together.

This song is in the style of an Israeli folk-dance.

Dona Dona

Words and Music by Sholom Secunda   English Words by Arthur Kevess and Teddi Schwartz

1. On a wag - on bound for mar - ket   there's a calf with a mourn - ful eye,
2. "Stop com - plain - ing," said the far - mer, "Who told you a ___ calf to be,
3. Calves are eas - i - ly bound and slaught - ered, nev - er know - ing the rea - son why,

High a - bove him there's a swal - low   wing - ing swift - ly ___ through the sky.
Why don't you_have wings to fly_with,   like the swal - low so proud and free?"
But who - ev - er trea - sures free - dom,   like the swal - low has learned to fly,

How the winds are laugh - ing,   They laugh with all their might.

Laugh and laugh the whole day through, and half the sum - mer's night.

Accelerando

Do-na, do-na, do-na, do-na,   Do-na, do-na, do-na, ___ don,

1. & 2.

Do-na, do-na, do-na, do-na,   Do-na, do-na, do-na, don.

3.

Do - na,   do - na,   do - na,   don.

The Violinist
Marc Chagall

161

Warming Up

If you go early to a sports event, you'll probably see players going through exercises that get their muscles ready for the game. Without these warm-up exercises, they will not play as well and they risk injuring muscles that are not prepared.

Musicians warm up their voices or instruments before beginning to make music. Here are some warm-up exercises.

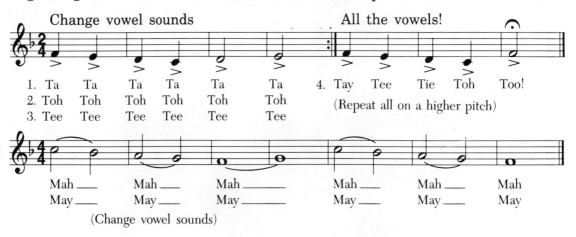

Change vowel sounds

All the vowels!

1. Ta Ta Ta Ta Ta Ta
2. Toh Toh Toh Toh Toh Toh
3. Tee Tee Tee Tee Tee Tee

4. Tay Tee Tie Toh Too!

(Repeat all on a higher pitch)

Mah —— Mah —— Mah ——— Mah —— Mah —— Mah
May —— May —— May ——— May —— May —— May

(Change vowel sounds)

Now that your voice is warmed up, here is a song to sing.

Charlottetown

Folk Song from Southern United States   Countermelody by Mary Hoffman

Countermelody

Char - lotte - town   is   burn —— ing,   burn - ing,

Melody

Char - lotte - town's   burn - ing down,   Good - bye,   good - bye,   Burn - ing down

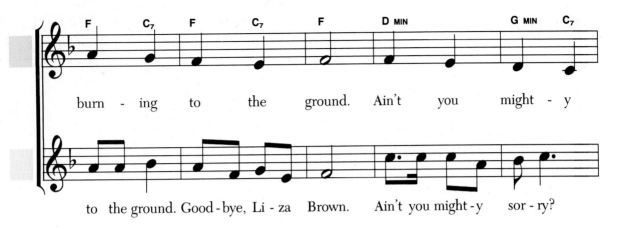

burn - ing to the ground. Ain't you might - y

to the ground. Good - bye, Li - za Brown. Ain't you might -y sor - ry?

sor - ry? Ain't you sor - ry, Li - za Brown?

Good - bye, good - bye. Ain't you might-y sor-ry? Good - bye, Li-za Brown.

Singing With Style

Different songs need different voices. The tone quality a singer chooses for a song can completely change the style. How will you decide on the tone quality and style for a song?

Look at this list of descriptive words. Then look at the list of songs. Which words best describe the vocal style for each song?

flowing, accented, jerky,
brassy, soft, loud,
rhythmic, legato, staccato,
crisp diction, smooth diction,

Mr. Touchdown, U.S.A.
I Got Rhythm
Waters Ripple and Flow
On the Road Again

Performing a Song

How should this song be sung? Use the melody line and words to decide how to use your voice. Where will you breathe? How do you think the words should be pronounced? Are there places where you would sing louder? Softer? In other words, how can you use your voice to interpret this song in the best possible way?

Peace Like a River

Traditional   Arranged by Larry Eisman

1. I've got peace like a riv-er, I've got peace like a

riv-er, I've got peace like a riv-er in my soul, _____ I've got
(in my soul)

peace like a riv-er, I've got peace like a riv-er, I've got

peace like a riv-er in my soul. _____
(in my soul.)

2. I've got joy like a fountain . . .   3. I've got love like the ocean . . .

Call Chart 5

9 *Singing Styles*

Singing well means singing a song in the style best suited to it. You can almost hear the style of singing when you look at these pictures of singers in performance.

1.

2.

3.

4.

Stage Movement

Sharing Music with an Audience

"I'll send an S. O. S. to the world."

Performing music in front of an audience means sharing the music with people who are watching and listening.

"I'll send an S. O. S. to the world."

Always know what you want to be doing with a song. Decide how you will stand or move or interpret the song. These performers seem to have found themselves on stage by accident.

Songs With Movement

Some songs work well with movement. If you are singing in a group, it is very effective if you make movements together.

"I've   got   rhy -   thm"

Other songs are more easygoing. The movements you make should reflect a smoother, more relaxed rhythm. But you can still move together.

"Mi - chael, row the boat ashore . . . ."

Making a Motion

Try making motions on important words or beats in the
music. However, you should always make the movements
natural and appropriate to the song. Crazy actions on the
stage can be a lot of fun for both the performers and the
audience, but even comical antics should be planned and
well-rehearsed.

"My string bass, my string bass, I LOVE to play my string bass."

You can "underline" important words in a song with motions.
Sometimes just bringing out a single word can be very effective.

"I've   got   STAR   -   light . . . ."

Mixed Movement

Sometimes everyone on the stage can be doing something different, and it can be fun to watch. Even this visible confusion should be well planned, however.

"Well, it's a good day for singin' a song . . . ."

Coordinated Movement

Movement that is coordinated, where everyone moves at the same time, is one of the best ways to make an audience pay attention.

"It's a good day from morn - in' till night."

A Song You Can Perform

In a World of Music

Words and Music by Linda Williams

1. There is a place I go, — built on a song, And if you
2. Riv - ers of mel - o - dy, — moun - tains of sound, rain - bows of

want to know, — Come a - long. _____ Not real - ly hard to find, —
har - mo - ny — all a - round. ____ Rooms full of rhy - thm and _

not ver - y far, Just lis - ten now, — do you know where _ you are? ____
if you want more, Well, an - y key _ will o - pen an - y door. ___

In a world, in a world of mu - sic, _____ In a world made of

rhy - thm and song. _____ I can bring you there, _ I can sing you there; _
(of song _)

In a world of mu - sic, That's where we be - long. ___

That's where we be - long. ___ I can bring you there, ___ I can sing you there; ___

In a world of mu - sic, That's where we be - long. ___

Making Contact

If you want an audience to pay attention to you, you must pay attention to them. Remember, for an audience, the most important part of your face is your eyes!

"And an - y key will o - pen an - y door . . . ."

Singing Concert Style

Whether you perform a song with motion and dancing, or just by standing still and singing, there is one thing to remember.

An audience is looking at you when you perform. Look at them. Smile at them as much as you can. You can have a happy face even when you are singing.

Sheep May Safely Graze

Music by J. S. Bach   English Words by Linda Williams

God, our shep-herd, in thy keep-ing, safe in thy care for all our days, God, our shep-herd, wak-ing, sleep-ing, Lead and guide us, Walk be-side us, So Thy sheep may safe-ly graze. So thy

1. Go on to next section
2. Fine

sheep may safe-ly graze.   graze.

Give us cour-age when we fal-ter; Ease the bur-dens we must bear. Let our hearts re-joice in thy lov-ing care.   Turn thy

face to shine ___ up-on us, ___ when the ___ storm-y wind ___ and

rain de - scend, ___ Be our _ shep - herd and friend. ___ No ___ harm _

poco rit.   D.S. al Fine

___ shall come to us with _ thee watch-ing o - ver _ us _ till _ jour-ney's _ end.

The Pirates of Penzance

William Schwenck Gilbert and Arthur Seymour Sullivan were English writers of a number of very famous operettas. Although they lived around 1900, during the time of Britain's Queen Victoria, their musical plays still delight audiences around the world. Mr. Gilbert wrote the words and Mr. Sullivan composed the music.

One of the most famous of all Gilbert and Sullivan musical plays is *The Pirates of Penzance*. You can learn some of the songs from this operetta. Listen to the *overture* to the play. It will set the mood of the story.

Overture to *Pirates of Penzance*

..........................Gilbert and Sullivan

The Story

A young man, Frederic, is an accidental pirate. When he was a lad, his nurse was told to apprentice him to a *pilot*. She misunderstood and made him a *pirate* instead. As he is an honorable young man, he will be true to his pirate comrades for the duration of his apprenticeship.

In fact, Frederic is a "slave of duty." He has vowed that on the day he reaches his twenty-first birthday, he will destroy the pirate band, and leave that life behind him.

Frederic's nurse, Ruth, who has been with him all these years, wants to leave the pirate ship and marry her young charge. However, Frederic meets and falls in love with Mabel, one of the daughters of the Major General.

This famous patter song introduces the Major General to the audience. By the end of the song, you know exactly the kind of person he is!

LISTENING SKILLS **10**

"A Modern Major General"
. . . . . . Gilbert and Sullivan

A Musical Introduction

The pirate band is led by a fierce
buccaneer, a Pirate King. However,
he is not nearly so terrible as he
describes himself in this song.

I Am a Pirate King

Words by W. S. Gilbert   Music by Sir Arthur Sullivan

1. Oh,   bet - ter far   to   live __ and die
2. When I   sal - ly forth to seek __ my prey   I

Un - der the brave black   flag I fly, Than play   a sanc - ti -
help my - self in a roy - al way; I sink   a few more

mo - nious part, With a pi - rate head and a   pi - rate heart.
ships, _ it's true, Than a well - bred mon - arch ought to do!

A - way to the cheat - ing world go   you,   Where
But ma - ny a king on   a first - class throne,   If he

pi - rates all ___ are well - to - do, But I'll be true to the
wants to call ___ his crown his own, Must man - age some - how

song I sing, And live ___ and die a Pi - rate King. For ___ I
to get through More dir - ty work than ever I do.

Chorus

am a Pi - rate King (You are! Hur - rah for the Pi - rate King) ___ And it

is, it is a glo - rious thing ___ To be a Pi - rate King! ___ For I

Chorus   *Solo*

am a Pi - rate King (You are! Hur - rah for our Pi - rate King!) ___ And it

Chorus

is, it is a glo - rious thing ___ To be a Pi - rate King! (It is! Hur -

All

rah for our Pi - rate King) Hur - rah for our Pi - rate King! ___

Sisters and Sweethearts

Unaware that the pirates are plotting their capture, the carefree sisters wander on the beach. When they notice that Mabel and Frederic are having a romantic conversation, they tactfully sing about the weather.

How Beautifully Blue the Sky

from *The Pirates of Penzance*

Words by W. S. Gilbert Music by Sir Arthur Sullivan

Mabel and Frederick (on repeat only)

ev - er mai - den wake from dream __ of

Chorus of Girls

How beau-ti-ful-ly blue the sky, The glass is ris-ing ver-y high, Con-

home - ly du - ty, To

tin-ue fine I hope it may, And yet it rained but yes-ter-day. To -

to ⊕

find her day - light break with such ___ ex -

second time to ⊕

mor-row it may rain a - gain, (I hear the coun-try wants some rain) Yet

peo - ple say, I know not why, That we shall have a

warm Ju - ly. To - mor-row it may pour a - gain, (I hear the coun-try
wants some rain) Yet peo-ple say, I know not why, That we shall have a

Mabel and Frederick

Did

ceed - ing beau - ty!

warm Ju - ly. How

peo-ple say, I know not why, That we shall have a

Ah, yes! _____

warm Ju - ly, Yet peo - ple say, I know not why, That we shall have a

Ah, yes, Ah, yes! _____

warm Ju - ly, a warm Ju - ly. _____

The Plot Thickens

The story is further complicated when Frederic discovers that he was born in leap year and has had only five birthdays. Now his sense of duty forbids him to leave the pirate band.

The pirates capture the girls and their father. But the clever Major General tells the pirates that he is a poor orphan. Out of sympathy, since the pirates are all orphans themselves, they let him go.

A band of policemen come to save the day. This song tells about the joy of battle. But like the pirates, they are not nearly as brave as they like to think they are!

Ta-Ran-Ta-Ra

Words by W. S. Gilbert   Music by Sir Arthur Sullivan

When the fore-man bares his steel,   We un-

Ta-ran - ta - ra,   ta-ran - ta-ra!

com - fort - a - ble feel!   And we

Ta - ran - ta - ra!

find the wis - est thing

Is to

Ta - ran - ta - ra, ta - ran - ta - ra!

slap our chests and sing Ta - ran - ta - ra!

For when

Ta - ran - ta - ra!

threat - en'd with e - meutes

And your

Ta - ran - ta - ra, ta - ran - ta - ra!

heart is in your boots,

There is

Ta - ran - ta - ra!

no - thing brings it round, Like the trum - pet's mar - tial sound, Like the

Solo and Chorus of Policemen

trum - pet's mar - tial sound. Ta - ran - ta - ra, ta - ran - ta -

Chorus of Girls

Go, ye

ra, ta - ran - ta - ra, ta - ran - ta - ra, ta - ran - ta - ra, ta - ran - ta -

he - roes, go to im - mor - ta - li - ty! Go, ye

ra, ta - ran - ta - ra, ta - ran - ta - ra, ta - ran - ta - ra, ta - ran - ta -

he - roes, go to im - mor - ta - li - ty! Tho' ye

ra!

Ta - ran - ta -

die in com - bat go - ry, Ye shall live in song and sto - ry; Go to

ra, ta-ran - ta-ra, ta-ran - ta - ra! _____

im - mor - ta - li - ty! _____

A Happy Ending

After many further complications in the plot, all turns out for the best. The pirates are reformed, the policemen have done their duty, and the Major General and his daughters are safe and sound.

Best of all, Mabel and Frederic are together at last, and are sure to live happily ever after!

183

Dance to the Music

Throughout the ages, dancing has had a strong impact on the music of the time.

The Jolly Flatboatmen
George Caleb Bingham

Dancing was important to the Greeks, and dance training was required as part of the standard education of the young people.

Dance—The Royal Treatment

In the Renaissance and Baroque courts, the noble lords and ladies loved to dance.

A stately dance called the *minuet* was introduced in the French court around 1670. Like other court dances, the minuet was based on a country dance, transformed by its regal setting. This familiar minuet by Bach is still popular in our own time.

 Minuet in G Major .... J. S. Bach

The Waltz King

Early in the 1800s in Austria, a man named Johann Strauss became famous for his waltzes.

Johann Strauss's son, who had the same name, carried on the family tradition. He became even more renowned than his father. He wrote so many famous waltzes that he was called The Waltz King. Listen to this famous waltz by the younger Strauss.

 "The Blue Danube" (excerpt) ... Johann Strauss Jr.

Country Dancing

The waltz had existed for a long time. It had been danced in the villages of Germany and Austria for longer than anyone could remember. The country version of this three-quarter-time dance was rough and vigorous.

The *Scherzo* movement of a symphony by Gustav Mahler is the style of these country dances.

 "Scherzo" from *Symphony No. 1* (excerpt)... Mahler

A New Song in the Old Tradition

Square dancing originated in America's early days.

The energy and high spirits of the traditional square dance can be heard in this song, which was written for a movie in 1947.

Country Style

Words and Music by Johnny Burke and James Van Heusen

When it comes to fan-cy dan-cin' or to mus-ic with a smile,
When it comes to arms that hold ya, Eyes that shine a-bout a mile,

Fan - cy dan - cin', Mus - ic with a smile,
Arms that hold ya, Eyes that shine a mile,

Clap:

Or to nice ro-man-cin', Make mine coun-try style.
Like I just now told ya, Make mine coun-try style.

Clap:

Or to nice ro-man-cin', — Make mine coun-try style.
Like I just now told ya, — Make mine coun-try style.

Solo first time
All second time

Hear that fid-dle! I could lis-ten all night.

All shout:

Hear that ban-jo! Ain't that some-thin'? All right!

1
Dance and share a lov-in' cup with dif-f'rent part-ners for a-while,

2
Dance with dif - f'rent part - ners for a-while,

Clap:

1
But for hitch - in' up with, Make mine coun-try style. *D.S.*

Clap:

2
But for hitch - in' up with, Make mine coun-try style. *D.S.*

last time

1
Make mine coun-try style. _____ *Shout:* All right!

last time

2
Make mine coun-try style. _____ *Shout:* All right!

Social Dancing in America

Most of the aristocrats in colonial America loved social dancing. Adults took lessons from "dancing masters," and they insisted that their children learn dancing as part of their general education.

Thomas Jefferson made a schedule for his daughter to practice dancing every other day from ten until one. John Quincy Adams wrote that he often danced from seven in the evening until four in the morning!

 Allemande . . . . Bach

THE ALLEMANDE DANCE.

New York Public Library, Dance Collection

188

A Polka from Our Century

There were numerous society balls during the 1800s. Many of the dances were performed in lines or sets. But the most popular dances were the waltz and the polka.

Here is a famous polka from the 1940s.

Pennsylvania Polka

Words and Music by Lester Lee and Zeke Manners

A Circle Dance

America has a rich cultural heritage, much of it borrowed from other countries. Our country has adopted the spirit, traditions, and dance patterns of a multitude of immigrants.

This song goes with a popular circle dance from Israel called the *Horah*.

Hava Nagila

Jewish Folk Song

u - ru a - chim b' - lev sa - me - ach, u - ru a - chim b' - lev sa - me - ach,
oo - roo ah - kheem buh - lev sah - meh - ah'kh oo - roo ah - kheem buh - lev sah - meh - ah'kh

u - ru a - chim, u - ru a - chim b'lev sa - me - ach.
oo - roo ah - kheem oo - roo ah - kheem b'lev sah - meh - ah'kh

The world heritage of Jewish song, poetry, and instrumental
music reaches back into the writings of the Old Testament.
Even the earth seems to dance to this joyous music.

O sing unto the Lord a new song. . . .
Make a joyful noise unto the Lord,
 all the earth:
Make a loud noise, and rejoice, and sing praise.

Sing unto the Lord with the harp;
With the harp, and the voice of a psalm.

With trumpets and sound of cornet
 make a joyful noise. . . .

Let the sea roar, and the fullness thereof;
The world, and they that dwell therein.

Let the floods clap their hands;
Let the hills be joyful together. . . .

—*from Psalm 98*

A Dance Style Made in America

Just as the music of black Americans was the seed for our truly American music, so it is with the dance. Even during the days of slavery, black people began to develop songs and dances that were distinctly theirs. This style was so powerful and exciting that it has had a worldwide and lasting effect on all music and dance as we know it.

Traditional African steps and body movements, combined with European set dances, evolved into something completely new. The popular dance style we call "tap" was invented by black artists.

John Bubbles

Some famous black dancers from the early
1900s were John Bubbles, Peg-Leg Bates—
who could do almost any dance step in spite
of his handicap—and Bill Robinson. Bill
"Bojangles" Robinson has often been called
the greatest tap dancer of all time.

Peg-Leg Bates

Bill Robinson

Dancing on Sand

The "soft shoe" was a dance style similar to tap. The dancer sprinkled sand on the sidewalk or the stage, and made percussive dance sounds by dancing on the sanded surface.

Soft Shoe Song

Words and Music by Roy Jordan and Sid Bass

Give me that old soft shoe, I said that old soft shoe. Ah -
one, ah - two, ah - doo-dle-dee doo-dle-dee doo.
Play me that old soft shoe and noth-in' else will do, That's the
kind of dance we used to do. We'll sing love's re - frain,
(Just like a vau-de-ville team) Dance the whole night through; *(Do-in' the cut-est rou-tine)*

Stroll-ing lov-er's lane, We'll har-mo-nize and
(Just like we're play-ing a scene)

Coda

doo-dle-dee doo-dle-dee-doo. Give me that else will do; Mis-ter

Lead-er, play the song and dance I love to do: the old
(I'm talk-in' a-bout the old)

soft *(I'm talk-in' a-bout the soft)* shoe. Soft shoe!

Dance Craze Days

During the twenty years between 1910 and 1930, Americans were dance crazy! Dance fads came and went with real 20th century speed.

There were *dance songs,* songs that gave instructions for steps and movements in the lyrics. There were dance *marathons.* Couples danced continuously until exhaustion forced them to stop. Sometimes they danced for several days. The last couple on their feet usually won a big prize.

The greatest dance craze of all was the Charleston. It became the dance sensation of the country when the chorus line of an all-black Broadway show, *Runnin' Wild,* danced to "Charleston."

Charleston

Words and Music by Cecil Mack and Jimmy Johnson

Charles - ton, _ Charles - ton, _ Made in _ Car-o - lin - a, _

Some dance, _ some prance, _ I'll say _ There's no-thing fin - er than the

Charles - ton, _ Charles - ton, _ Oh, how _ you can shuf - fle, _

Ev-'ry step _ you do leads to some - thing new, Man, I'm tell - ing you

It's a la - pa-zoo! Buck dance, _ wing dance, _ will be _ a back

num - ber, _ but the Charles - ton, _ the new Charles - ton, _ That dance _ is

sure-ly a com - er, Some - time _____ you'll _ dance it one time, _

The dance _ called the Charles - ton, _ made in South _ Car-o - line. ___

Dancing Gets a New Twist

During the 1930s a dance called the Fox Trot replaced the waltz for ballroom dancing. For the younger, more casual dance crowd, one popular dance was the more athletic Lindy. But only a few years later, in the 1940s, America began to jitterbug! Using the patterns of the Fox Trot and the Lindy, the jitterbug dancers improvised and developed hundreds of variations. These were often spectacular turns, jumps, lifts, and spins.

Then came Rock and Roll!
Black musicians had been playing and recording this music for more than fifty years, but it was not until the 1950s that the rest of the world discovered it.

One early dance that was done to Rock and Roll music was the Twist. The song was composed in the late 1950s, but when it was introduced by Chubby Checker in 1960 it became a new dance craze.

The Twist

Words and Music by Frank Ballard

Song and Dance—American Musical Theater

America has given birth to a special kind of popular musical theater. It grew out of the European opera and operetta.

In 1943 came the landmark musical, *Oklahoma!* The songs were in the popular style but were used to develop the characters and set the scenes.

Listen to a recording of the final scene from *Oklahoma*.

Oklahoma (Finale) ..... Rodgers and Hammerstein

American musical shows have gained enormous popularity worldwide. They are even performed in other languages.

Test 5

Here are some songs that might be performed, either in the classroom or in public. Each song is useful in a different way. Read the descriptions, and then decide which song fits the description. Put the letter in the blank space.

A. Bye-Bye, Blues
B. Dona Dona
C. I Am a Pirate King
D. Sheep May Safely Graze

E. In a World of Music
F. I Got Rhythm
G. I Am a Great Musician

1. _____ A song that tells a story. It must be sung clearly and carefully, especially as it speeds up at the end.

2. _____ A song from a musical play. It has both solo and chorus parts, and introduces a colorful character.

3. _____ A song with long notes. It should be carefully sung in order to make smooth phrases.

4. _____ A comical song with several solos. It can be sung with stage movement to describe various instruments.

5. _____ A lively song by George Gershwin. It can be performed with rhythmic stage movements on important words.

6. _____ A beautiful concert-style song. It should be sung simply and as beautifully as possible.

7. _____ A song about making music. With or without movements it is a good song to share with an audience.

Test 6

Here are three categories, A, B, and C. Each has words which describe a singing and performing style.

A	B	C
Jazzy	Humorous	Lyrical
Accented	Dance-like	Calm
Cheerful	Lively	Smooth lines
Rhythmic	Full of motion	Quieter mood

Here is a list of songs from your book. Choose the category that fits each song *best*. Put the letter of that category (A, B, or C) in the space next to the song title.

_____ The Twist

_____ Peace Like a River

_____ Ta-Ran-Ta-Ra

_____ In a World of Music

_____ Sheep May Safely Graze

_____ Dona Dona

_____ Country Style

_____ I Got Rhythm

_____ I Am a Great Musician

_____ Bonnie Doon

I Like Music

Words and Music by Carmino Ravosa

Guitar:

Student: I am music. I make the world weep, laugh, wonder, and worship.

Student: Music is one of our great material needs. We need food, clothing, shelter—and we need music!

Student: Singing makes the heartache easier, lifts the spirits, makes the work go faster.

Student: Singing makes us feel good. Even when we are sad, a song can make us feel better.

Speaker: People don't sing because they're happy . . . .

All: They're happy because they sing!

People Don't Sing Because They're Happy 🔟

Words and Music by Carmino Ravosa

Student: We know music is good for us. Aldous Huxley said, "After silence, that which comes nearer to the inexpressible is music."

Student: Someone else once said, "Music is another planet."

Student: Goethe said, "A man should hear a little music, read a little poetry, and see a fine picture every day of his life."

Student: You can read a poem or look at a fine picture, but music is different. It isn't there unless somebody *makes* it. You have to sing it, play it, or dance it. You've got to really get into the music, pass the melody into the beat. (Begins snapping fingers)

Student: The beat! (picks up finger snaps) Do you know what rhythm is?

All: No, what?

Student: If you have to ask . . . . you haven't got it!

You've Got to Get into the Music

Words and Music by Carmino Ravosa

Student: Now, wait a minute! The beat and the rhythm are important, but it is the melody that is most difficult to write. Haydn said, "The invention of a fine melody is a work of genius."

Student: Do you know, there are no books to tell you how to write a melody, or even what a good melody *is*. But you know one when you hear it.

Student: A famous composer once said, "If a man would know me, let him find me in my music."

Student: Heinrich Heine said, "Where words leave off, music begins."

Student: Words and music—rhythm and melody—Do you know what's missing?

All: Harmony!

Student: Right! Now, put it all together . . . and let's make music.

Let's Make Music 🔟

Words and Music by Carmino Ravosa

Let's make mu - sic,   You   and   me. _____
Let's make love - ly   Har - mo -

Let's make mu - sic,   You   and   me. _____
Let's make love - ly   Har - mo -

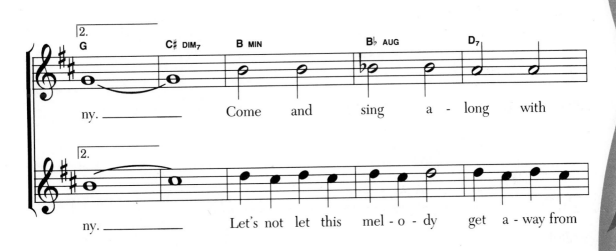

ny. _____   Come   and   sing   a - long   with

ny. _____   Let's not let this mel - o - dy   get   a - way from

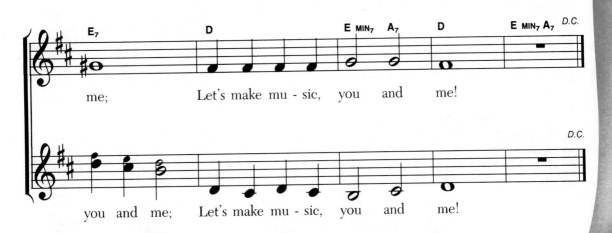

me;   Let's make mu - sic,   you   and   me!

you and me;   Let's make mu - sic,   you   and   me!

Student: "Music is the shorthand of emotion." That's what Tolstoy said.

Student: Some say music is love in search of a word. Others say music is love itself.

Student: Everyone has a different opinion. But this we know. Music is in a continual state of *becoming.* Each person brings something different to a piece of music. Each person gets something different out of it.

Student: If there's music in us, we should express it. Oliver Wendell Holmes said, "Alas for those who never sing, but die with their music in them."

Student: If there's music in you, let it out!

If There's Music in You

Words and Music by Carmino Ravosa

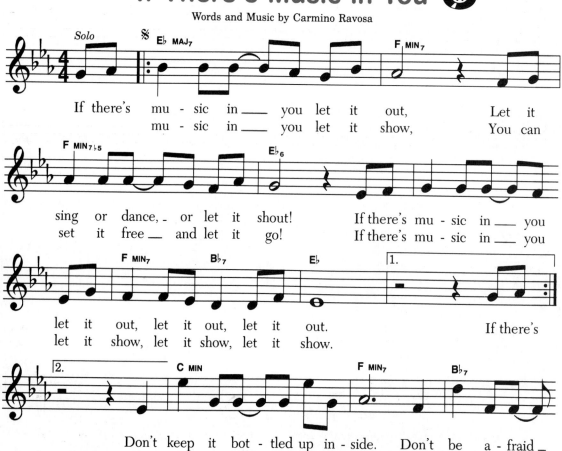

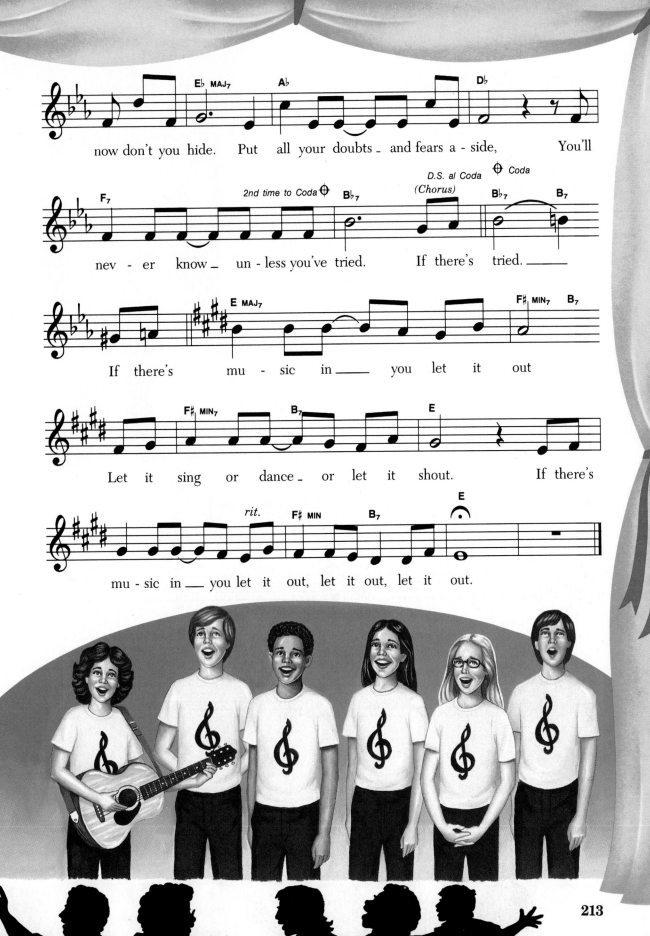

Student: I shot an arrow into the air,
It fell to earth, I knew not where.

All: For so swiftly it flew the sight
Could not follow in its flight.

Student: I breathed a song into the air,
It fell to earth, I knew not where.

All: For who has sight so keen and strong,
That it can follow the flight of song.

Student: Long, long afterward, in an oak,
I found the arrow, still unbroke.

All: And the song, from beginning to end,
I found again . . . .

Student: In the heart of a friend.

I Am Music

Words and Music by Carmino Ravosa

1. *Solo* I am mu - sic, sing me. With it life you bring me, sing me.
2. *Full Chorus*

I am mu - sic, play me. Do not talk or say me, play me.

I am noth - ing much to see, _____ It's you that's gon - na make me, me.

I am mu-sic, hear me. All your life be near me, and hear me.

hear me. _____ I like mu - sic, __

An-y kind of mu - sic __ I like mu-sic, yes I do. __

Turn to "I Like Music," page 205, and finish the song:

I like music, any kind of music,
I like music, yes I do!

Music can make me feel happy,
Music can make me sad.
Music can make me sing and dance,
Music can make me glad that

I like music, any kind of music,
I like music, yes I do.
I like music, any kind of music,
I like music, yes I do!

Jan	1 2 3 4 5 6	Jul	1 2 3 4 5 6
	7 8 9 10 11 12 13 14 15		7 8 9 10 11 12 13 14 15
	16 17 18 19 20 21 22 23 24		16 17 18 19 20 21 22 23 24
	25 26 27 28 29 30 31		25 26 27 28 29 30 31
Feb	1 2 3 4 5 6	Aug	1 2 3 4 5 6
	7 8 9 10 11 12 13 14 15		7 8 9 10 11 12 13 14 15
	16 17 18 19 20 21 22 23 24		16 17 18 19 20 21 22 23 24
	25 26 27 28		25 26 27 28 29 30 31
Mar	1 2 3 4 5 6	Sep	1 2 3 4 5 6
	7 8 9 10 11 12 13 14 15		7 8 9 10 11 12 13 14 15
	16 17 18 19 **20** 21 22 23 24		16 17 18 19 20 21 22 23 24
	25 26 27 28 29 30 31		25 26 27 28 29 30
Apr	1 2 3 4 5 6	Oct	1 2 3 4 5 6
	7 8 9 10 11 12 13 14 15		7 8 9 10 11 12 13 14 15
	16 17 18 19 20 21 22 23 24		16 17 18 19 20 21 22 23 24
	25 26 27 28 29 30		25 26 27 28 29 30 31
May	1 2 3 4 5 6	Nov	1 2 3 4 5 6
	7 8 9 10 11 12 13 14 15		7 8 9 10 11 12 13 14 15
	16 17 18 19 20 21 22 23 24		16 17 18 19 20 21 22 23 24
	25 26 27 28 29 30		25 26 27 28 29 30
Jun	1 2 3 4 5 6	Dec	1 2 3 4 5 6
	7 8 9 10 11 12 13 14 15		7 8 9 10 11 12 13 14 15
	16 17 18 19 20 21 22 23 24		16 17 18 19 20 21 22 23 24
	25 26 27 28 29 30		25 26 27 28 29 30 31

217

Young Citizens of the World

"I Am But a Small Voice" is a song to sing anytime, but you might want to save it for a special occasion!

I Am But a Small Voice

Original Words by Odina E. Batnay   English Words and Music by Roger Whittaker

© 1983 Tembo Music, Canada (CAPAC). Used by permission.

Barter

Life has loveliness to sell,
   All beautiful and splendid things,
Blue waves whitened on a cliff,
   Soaring fire that sways and sings,
And children's faces looking up
Holding wonder like a cup.

Life has loveliness to sell,
   Music like a curve of gold,
Scent of pine trees in the rain,
   Eyes that love you, arms that hold,
And for your spirit's still delight,
Holy thoughts that star the night.

Spend all you have for loveliness,
   Buy it and never count the cost;
For one white singing hour of peace
   Count many a year of strife well lost,
And for a breath of ecstasy
Give all you have been, or could be.

Sara Teasdale

Our National Anthem

Our national anthem is an expression of victory over enemies of freedom.

The Star-Spangled Banner

Words by Francis Scott Key   Music by John Stafford Smith

1. Oh, — say! can you see, by the dawn's ear-ly light, What so
2. On the shore, dim-ly seen through the mists of the deep, Where the
3. Oh, — thus be it ever when — free men shall stand Be -

proud-ly we hailed at the twi-light's last gleam-ing, Whose broad
foe's haugh-ty host in dread si-lence re-pos-es, What is
tween their loved homes and the war's des-o-la-tion! Blest with

stripes and bright stars, through the per-il-ous fight, O'er the
that which the breeze, o'er the tow-er-ing steep, As it
vic-t'ry and peace, may the heav'n-res-cued land Praise the

ram-parts we watched were so gal-lant-ly stream-ing? And the
fit-ful-ly blows, half con-ceals, half dis-clos-es? Now it
Pow'r that hath made and pre-served us a na-tion! Then —

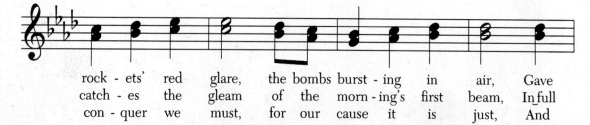

rock-ets' red glare, the bombs burst-ing in air, Gave
catch-es the gleam of the morn-ing's first beam, In full
con-quer we must, for our cause it is just, And

220

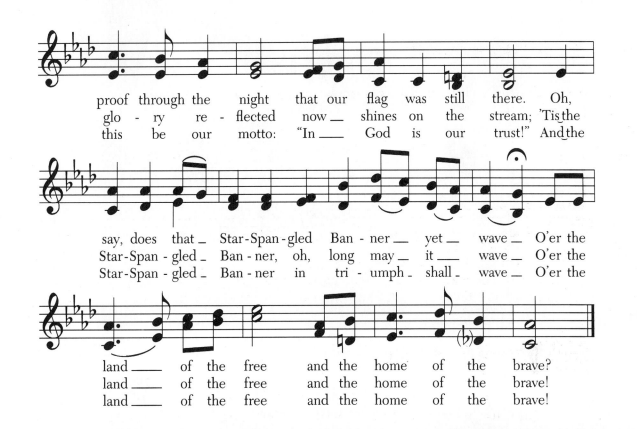

proof through the night that our flag was still there. Oh,
glo - ry re - flected now __ shines on the stream; 'Tis the
this be our motto: "In __ God is our trust!" And the

say, does that __ Star-Span-gled Ban-ner __ yet __ wave __ O'er the
Star-Span - gled __ Ban-ner, oh, long may __ it __ wave __ O'er the
Star-Span - gled __ Ban-ner in tri - umph __ shall __ wave __ O'er the

land ____ of the free and the home of the brave?
land ____ of the free and the home of the brave!
land ____ of the free and the home of the brave!

From Sea to Shining Sea

America, the Beautiful

Words by Katharine Lee Bates   Music by Samuel A. Ward

1. O beau - ti - ful for spa - cious skies, For am - ber waves of grain,
2. O beau - ti - ful for pil - grim feet, Whose stern im - pas - sioned stress
3. O beau - ti - ful for pa - triot dream That sees be - yond the years

For pur - ple moun - tain maj - es - ties A - bove the fruit - ed plain!
A thor - ough - fare for free - dom beat A - cross the wil - der - ness!
Thine al - a - bas - ter cit - ies gleam, Un - dimmed by hu - man tears!

A - mer - i - ca! A - mer - i - ca! God shed His grace on thee
A - mer - i - ca! A - mer - i - ca! God mend thine ev - 'ry flaw,
A - mer - i - ca! A - mer - i - ca! God shed His grace on thee

And crown thy good with broth - er - hood From sea to shin - ing sea!
Con - firm thy soul in self - con - trol, Thy li - ber - ty in law!
And crown thy good with broth - er - hood From sea to shin - ing sea!

America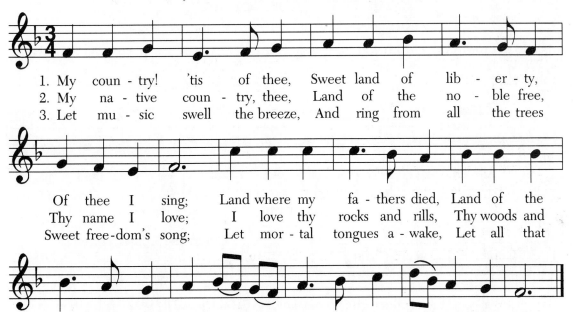

Words by Samuel Francis Smith   Music by Henry Carey

1. My coun - try! 'tis of thee, Sweet land of lib - er - ty,
2. My na - tive coun - try, thee, Land of the no - ble free,
3. Let mu - sic swell the breeze, And ring from all the trees

Of thee I sing; Land where my fa - thers died, Land of the
Thy name I love; I love thy rocks and rills, Thy woods and
Sweet free-dom's song; Let mor - tal tongues a - wake, Let all that

Pil - grims' pride, From ev - 'ry moun - tain - side Let free - dom ring!
tem - pled hills; My heart with rap - ture thrills Like that a - bove.
breathe par - take, Let rocks their si - lence break, The sound pro - long.

4. Our father's God, to Thee, Author of liberty,
    To Thee we sing;
    Long may our land be bright with Freedom's holy light
    Protect us by Thy might, Great God, our King!

Autumn Colors

Here is a Halloween song that tells about the warm colors and the cold chill of the autumn season.

Halloween Moon

Words and Music by Jean Riddle

Guitar:

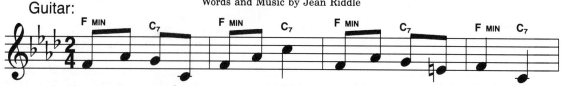

1. Brown Oc - to - ber grow-ing old, Sum - mer far be - hind us;
2. Hands and toes be - gin to freeze, Chil - ly winds are sigh - ing;
3. Prowl - ing in the dark of night When the ghosts are wak - ing;

All the leaves are red and gold Hal - low - een will find us
Some - one cries, he thinks he sees Owls and witch - es fly - ing
Quiv - er - ing with cold and fright, Shiv - er - ing and shak - ing,

Walk - ing in the au - tumn cold; May - be we'll see it soon:
Out a - cross the au - tumn trees; May - be we'll see it soon:
How we need your sil - ver light! May - be we'll see it soon:

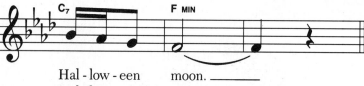

Hal - low - een moon. _____
Hal - low - een moon. _____
Hal - low - een moon. _____

Harvest time in the fall is traditionally a time of feasting and celebrating in many countries. In America, we mark the passing of the growing season with the feast of Thanksgiving.

Come, Ye Thankful People, Come

Words by Henry Alford   Music by George J. Elvey

1. Come, ye thank-ful peo-ple, come, Raise the song of har-vest home;
2. All the bless-ings of the field, All the stores the gar-dens yield;

All is safe-ly gath-ered in, Ere the win-ter storms be-gin;
All the fruits in full sup-ply, Rip-ened 'neath the sum-mer sky;

God, our Mak-er, doth pro-vide For our wants to be sup-plied;
All that Spring with boun-teous hand Scat-ters o'er the smil-ing land;

Come to God's own tem-ple, come, Raise the song of har-vest home.
All that lib-'ral au-tumn pours From her rich o'er-flow-ing stores.

Festival of Lights

The celebration of Chanukah,
the Jewish Festival of Lights,
takes place on late fall dates
that vary from year to year.

O Chanukah

Jewish Folk Song   English Words by Judith Eisenstein

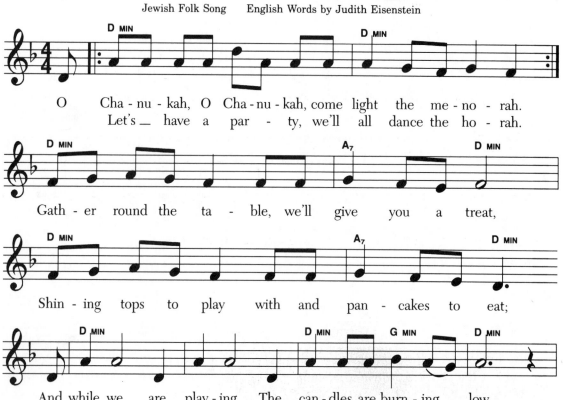

O Cha-nu-kah, O Cha-nu-kah, come light the me-no-rah.
Let's have a par-ty, we'll all dance the ho-rah.

Gath-er round the ta-ble, we'll give you a treat,

Shin-ing tops to play with and pan-cakes to eat;

And while we are play-ing, The can-dles are burn-ing low,

One for each night, they shed a sweet light to re-

1. mind us of days long a-go,

2. mind us of days long a-go.

From *Gateways To Jewish Song* collected and translated by Judith Eisenstein. Used by permission.

A favorite part of the holiday is the lighting of the candles of the menorah, one candle on each of the eight nights of Chanukah.

Around About Chanukah

Words and Music by David Eddleman

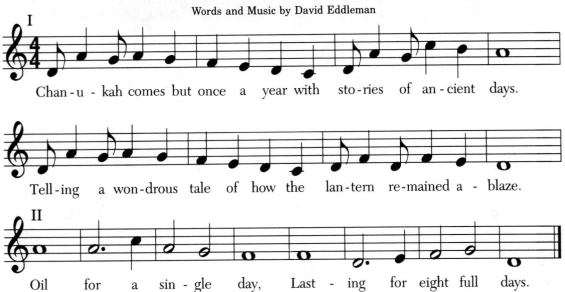

Chan-u-kah comes but once a year with sto-ries of an-cient days.

Tell-ing a won-drous tale of how the lan-tern re-mained a-blaze.

Oil for a sin-gle day, Last - ing for eight full days.

Accompany this round with a rhythm pattern on the tambourine:

A Song for Snowy Weather

Some parts of our country never see snow. But this is a favorite winter song even where the sun shines all year.

Winter Wonderland

Words by Dick Smith   Music by Felix Bernard

1. Sleigh-bells ring,   are you lis-t'nin'?   In the lane   snow is
2. Gone   a-way   is the blue-bird,   Here to stay   is a
3. When   it snows,   ain't it thrill-in'?   Tho' your nose   gets a

glis-t'nin',   A beau-ti-ful sight, _ We're hap-py to-night, _
new bird,   He's sing-ing a song _ as we go a-long, _
chill-in',   We'll frol-ic and play _ the Es-ki-mo way, _

1.,3.   Fine   *2.*

Walk-in' in   a win-ter won-der-land!   land!

In   the mead-ow we   can build   a snow-man,

And pre-tend that he's a cir-cus clown;   We'll have lots of fun with Mis-ter

D.C. al Fine

Snow-man,   Un-til   the oth-er kid-dies knock 'im down!

(To verse 3)

Play this Bell Part with "Winter Wonderland":

Let us walk in the white snow
   In a soundless space;
With footsteps quiet and slow
   At a tranquil pace
     Under veils of white lace.

We shall walk in velvet shoes:
     Wherever we go
Silence will fall like dews
     On white silence below.
     We shall walk in the snow.

from "Velvet Shoes"
by Elinor Wylie

A Holiday Tradition

We Wish You a Merry Christmas

English Carol

1. We wish you a mer-ry Christ-mas, We wish you a mer-ry Christ-mas,

We wish you a mer-ry Christ-mas, And a hap-py New Year!

2. Now bring us some figgy pudding . . .
   And bring it out here.

3. We won't go until we get some . . .
   So bring some out here.

4. We wish you a merry Christmas . . .
   And a happy New Year!

Bells

Descant

2. Now   bring   us   some   fig - gy   pud - ding,   Some
4. We   wish   you   a   mer - ry   Christ - mas,   A

fig - gy   pud - ding,   And   bring   it   out   here.
mer - ry   Christ - mas   and a   hap - py   New   Year.

230

A Beloved Carol

Silent Night

Words by Joseph Mohr   Music by Franz Gruber

Si - lent night,   ho - ly night,   All   is   calm,
Stil - le Nacht,   Hei - li - ge Nacht,   Al - les schläft,
No - che de paz,   no - che de a - mor,   To - do duerme en

all   is   bright   Round   yon   Vir - gin   Moth - er and Child.
ein - sam wacht   Nur das trau - te hoch - hei - li - ge Paar.
de - rre - dor.   Entre los as - tros que es - par - cen su luz,

Ho - ly In - fant so   ten - der and mild,   Sleep   in heav - en - ly
Hol - der Kna - be im   lok - ki - gen Haar,   schlaf' in himm - lisch - er
Bella a - nun - cian - do al ni - ñi - to Je - sús,   Brilla la es - tre - lla de

peace, ___   Sleep ___ in heav - en - ly   peace. ___
Ruh, ___   schlaf' ___ in himm - lisch - er   Ruh. ___
paz, ___   Bri - lla la es - tre - lla de   paz. ___

A French Carol

Bring a Torch, Jeannette, Isabella

17th Cent. French Carol   Arranged by Linda Williams

is	the	moth - er,	Ah!	Ah!	Beau - ti - ful	is	her	son. _____
is	the	moth - er,	Ah!	Ah!	Beau - ti - ful	is	her	child. _____

is the moth - er, Ah! Ah! Beau - ti - ful is her child. _____

This traditional carol from France is a favorite in many countries
of the world. The lower voices sing a harmony part that is like
another melody.

From England

This English carol has a second part that is like a separate melody for the lower voices.

The First Nowell

Traditional English Carol

1. The first Nowell the angel did say Was to
   fields where they lay keeping their sheep On a

cer-tain poor shep-herds in fields as they lay; In
cold win-ter's night that was so deep.

REFRAIN *Countermelody*

Now - ell, Now - ell, Now - ell, Now - ell,

Melody

Now - ell, Now - ell, Now - ell, Now - ell

Born is the King of Is - ra - el.

Born is the King of Is - ra - el.

2. They looked up and saw a star Shining in the East beyond them afar,
   And to the earth it gave great light, And so it continued both day and night.
   Refrain

234

A Chilly Round

The sound of a cold winter wind blows through this round. The repeated "wind and snow" sounds as chilly as this old etching.

Wind and Snow 🎵11

Words and Music by Joseph Fisch

Win-ter, win-ter, ice on the win-dow, Wind and snow, cold and blow-ing

wind and snow. Can-dles glow-ing, light-ing a win-ter hol-i-day.

Come out of the wind and snow, By the warm fire ___ come and stay.

Christmas Bells

This carol has a countermelody for the *higher* voices.

Ding-Dong Merrily on High

French Carol   English Words by G. R. Woodward   Arranged by Linda Williams

Countermelody

G   D₇   G   C   D₇

3. Ding-dong   mer-ri-ly,   in   heav'n   the

Melody

1.,3. Ding-dong! mer-ri-ly on high   in heav'n the bells are
2. Pray you, du-ti-ful-ly prime   your mat-in chime, ye

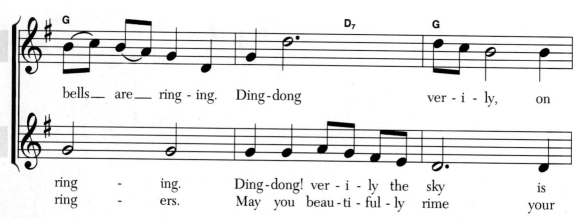

G   D₇   G

bells___ are___ ring-ing. Ding-dong   ver-i-ly,   on

ring   -   ing.   Ding-dong! ver-i-ly the sky   is
ring   -   ers.   May you beau-ti-ful-ly rime   your

C   D₇   G

high   the   an-gel___ sing-ing. Glo   -   ri -

riv'n with an-gel sing   -   ing.   Glo   -   -
eve-time song, ye sing   -   ers.

a, Glo - ri - a Glo - ri - a, Ho -

san - na, ho - san - na _____ in ex - cel - sis!

- - - - ri - a, Ho - san - na in ex - cel - sis!

Green Leaves for Christmas

This beautiful carol has been a favorite
for many centuries.

The Holly and the Ivy

Traditional English Carol   Arranged by Mary Hoffman

Guitar:

1. The hol-ly and the i - vy, when they are both full
grown, of __ all the trees that are in the wood, the __ hol - ly bears the
crown; The ris - ing of the sun, __ and the run - ning of the
deer; The __ play-ing of the mer - ry pipes, sweet __ sing-ing in the

I (Higher voices)

choir. 2. The hol - ly bears a blos - som, as white as li - ly
hol - ly bears a ber - ry, as red as an - y

II (Lower voices, tacet verse 2, sing verse 3)

choir. 2. 𝄽 *(Tacet)*
hol - ly bears a ber - ry, as red as an - y

238

A New Song for the Holidays

A young student in an Illinois grade school wrote a poem about the holiday season. Her music teacher liked the poem so much that she set it to music.

Sounds of Christmas

Music by D. L. Brubaker   Based on a poem by Jenny Delaney

241

A Very Old Carol

"Gabriel's Message" is an ancient Basque carol that is still often sung in England. Although it mentions Christmas, it is actually a carol for a Christian holy day that comes in the early springtime.

After you learn the song, you may want to add some simple percussion parts. The little drum, finger cymbals, and tambourine are typical of medieval and renaissance music.

Gabriel's Message

Basque Carol   Words by Sabine Baring-Gould

1. The an - gel Ga - bri - el from hea - ven came, ___
2. "For know a bless - ed Moth - er thou shalt be, ___
3. Of her, Em-man - u - el, the child was born, ___
4. The an - gel Ga - bri - el from hea - ven came, ___

His wings as drift - ed snow, his eyes ___ as flame; ___
All gen - er - a - tions laud and hon - or thee, ___
In Beth - le - hem, all on a Christ - mas morn, ___
His wings as drift - ed snow, his eyes ___ as flame, ___

"All hail," said he, "thou low - ly maid - en Ma - ry, ___
Thy son shall be Em - man - u - el, by seers fore - told, ___
And ev - 'ry where through - out the world the peo - ple say, ___
"All hail," said he, "thou low - ly maid - en Ma - ry," ___

"Most high - ly fa - vored la - dy," Glo - ri - a!

Percussion Parts

These parts may be used one at a time with different verses of the song, or all at once. You may want to design your own routine.

Small Hand Drum (softly)

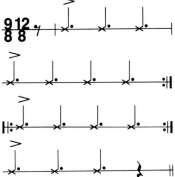

Finger Cymbals (♩⌒: "let ring")

Tambourine (very soft)

Be My Valentine

This old song can be decorated with a little countermelody.
Play it on the bells or any other melody instrument.

Heart of My Heart

Words and Music by Ben Ryan

Guitar:

"Heart of My Heart," I love that mel - o - dy, "Heart of My Heart," brings

back a mem - o - ry. When we were kids on the cor-ner of the street,

We were rough and read - y guys, But Oh! How we could har - mon - ize,

"Heart of My Heart," meant friends were dear-er then, Too bad we had to

part._____ I know a tear would glis - ten if once more I could

lis - ten To that gang that sang "Heart of My Heart." _____

COUNTERMELODY

A Song About Love

As you sing this song, you will see that the words are about a special kind of love.

Everybody Needs Love

Words and Music by Grace Bradford

Guitar:

Ev-'ry-bod-y needs love, ev-'ry-bod-y needs hap-pi-ness. _
Ev-'ry-bod-y needs praise, ev-'ry-bod-y needs sun - shine. _

Ev-'ry-bod-y needs joy, _____ ev-'ry-bod-y needs sweet suc-cess. _
Ev-'ry-bod-y needs con-fi-dence, _ ev-'ry-bod-y needs peace of mind. _

Well, I've searched the world o-ver, _ And the mes-sage is the same. _____
Well, I've searched the world o-ver, _ From the o-cean to the skies a-bove. _

Ev-'ry-bod-y says love _____ is the name of the game.
Ev-'ry-bod-y says loud and clear that the mes-sage is love.

Love _ will bring you hap-pi-ness, _ Love _ will bring you

sweet suc-cess. _ Love _ will give you con-fi-dence, _ Love. ___

A Change of Seasons

This beautiful Spanish-American song describes the coming of spring. Sing *"La primavera"* ("Springtime") in both Spanish and English.

Many Spanish songs use "Ay" the way "Oh" is used in English.

Springtime
(La primavera)

Spanish Folk Song from California   English Words by Linda Williams

At last comes the spring, the sea-son so ____ full of
Ya vie-ne la pri - ma-ve-ra, sem - bran-do
yah vyeh-neh lah pree - mah-veh-rah sehm - brahn-doh

flow-ers, so ____ full of flow-ers, ay, ay! And now ev-'ry
flo-res, sem - bran-do flo-res, ay, ay! Y ya los cam-
floh-rehs sehm - brahn-doh floh-res ahee ahee ee yah lohs kahm-

field is paint-ed so ____ man-y col-ors, so ____ man-y
pos se es-mal-tan de ____ mil co - lo-res, de ____ mil co-
pohs saiehs-mahl-tahn deh meel koh-loh-rehs deh meel koh-

col - ors. ____ Song - birds are sing - ing, ____
lo - res. ____ Can - tan las a - ves, ____
loh - rehs kahn - tahn lahs ah - vehs

248

Sweet _____ voic - es ring - ing, _____
Can - *tan* *las* *a* - *ves,* _____
kahn - tahn lah ah - vehs

Soft - ly ech - o - ing hills re - sound _____ in the
Los *o* - *te* - *ros* *re* - *pi* - *tan* *sus* _____ *tri* - *nos*
lohs oh - teh - rohs reh - pee - tahn soos tree - nohs

spring - time, *La* _____ *pri* - *ma* - *ve* - *ra.* _____
sua - *ves,* *sus* _____ *tri* - *nos* *sua* - *ves.* _____
swah - vehs soos tree - nohs swah - vehs

A Spring Festival

Purim is a traditional Jewish holiday that comes in springtime. Children dress in costumes and make as much noise as they possibly can!

This song for the Purim holiday describes the sound of the *greger,* a hand-held spinning noisemaker that goes "rash, rash, rash."

Purim Day 12

Traditional Melody   Hebrew Verse by L. Kipnis   English Words by Dav ben Shmuel

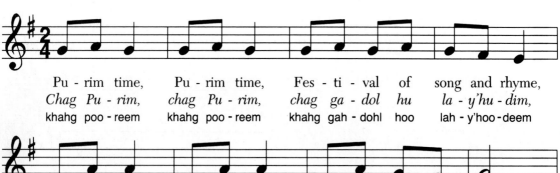

Pu - rim time,   Pu - rim time,   Fes - ti - val   of   song and rhyme,
Chag Pu - rim,   chag Pu - rim,   chag ga - dol   hu   la - y'hu - dim,
khahg poo - reem   khahg poo - reem   khahg gah - dohl   hoo   lah - y'hoo - deem

Wear a mask,   hap - py task,   hap - py hol - i - day.
Ma - se - chot,   ra - sha - nim,   z'mi - rot,   ri - ku - dim.
mah - sai - khoht   rah - shah - neem   zmee - roht   ree - koo - deem

Sound of the gre - ger, rash, rash, rash,   Sound of the gre - ger, rash, rash, rash,
Ha - va nar - i - sha, rash, rash, rash,   Ha - va nar - i - sha, rash, rash, rash,
hah - vah nahr - ee - shah rahsh rahsh rahsh   hah - vah nahr - ee - shah rahsh rahsh rahsh

Sound of the gre - ger,   rash, rash, rash,   Sing for Pu - rim Day.
Ha - va nar - i - sha,   rash, rash, rash,   ba - ra - sha - nim.
Hah - vah nahr - ee - shah   rahsh rahsh rahsh   bah - rah - shah - neem

250

A Popular Spring Song

April Showers

Words by B. G. DeSylva   Music by Louis Silvers

Though A-pril show-ers may come your way, they bring the flow-ers

that bloom in May; So if it's rain - ing, _____ have no re -

grets _____ be - cause it is - n't rain - ing rain you know, it's

rain - ing vi - o - lets. And where you see clouds up - on the hills,

you soon will see crowds of daf - fo - dils;

So keep on look - ing for a blue - bird and lis - t'ning for his

song, when - ev - er A - pril show - ers come a - long.

Can You Read This?

Yes, It's a good day for singin' a song,
And it's a good day for movin' along . . .

You can read the words. You have learned that the letters stand for certain sounds. Music can also be read when you know the kinds of sounds that are represented by the symbols on the page.

You can begin to "hear" the sound in your mind in the same way you do when you see a written word.

Begin With Rhythm

Musical symbols tell you whether notes are long or short.

Clap these patterns:

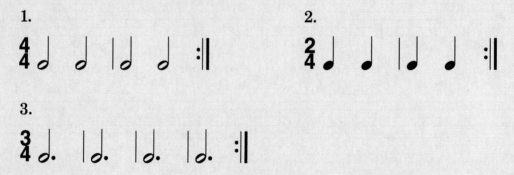

Notes have *time value* that you can read.

Clap this pattern of mixed time values:

Add More Musical Symbols

Add a musical staff  and you can give the rhythm
patterns different pitches. You can read a melodic line. Clap
the rhythm pattern of this music, then try singing the pitches
in rhythm. Notice whether the music moves up or down or
stays the same.

5.

Example 4 moved *by step* or repeated the same tones. Some
melodic lines move *by leap*. Read this melody that has leaps
between notes. All of the leaps are the same distance apart.

6.

This ostinato has leaps of different sizes.

7.

Here is a longer melody with both steps and leaps.

8.

A Musical Challenge

This melody is more complicated than the shorter ostinato patterns. However, if you study it one section at a time, it will be easier to read. Always begin by clapping the rhythm.

9.

Here is a melody with a rhythm pattern in $\frac{3}{4}$. Put *accents* on the first beat of each measure, even when you clap the pattern. It will make the music "dance."

10.

This melody will "march" in a $\frac{4}{4}$ rhythm. There are many leaps in the melody, but you can watch for repeated patterns, and it will be easier.

11.

A Musical Map

Written music can be very simple, or it can be full of
confusing signs. There can be roadblocks, detours and turns.
Watch the signs!

12.

This melody is like a curvy road. Clap the rhythm first, then
take it one section at a time. If you learn it slowly, then you
can sing it with the recording *up to tempo*. You can follow the
curves and not fall off the road!

13.

Playing the Guitar

This is how the neck of the guitar looks when you are holding it in playing position.

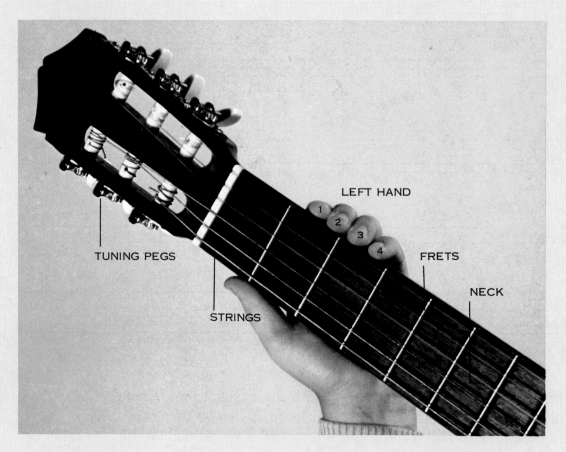

TUNING PEGS

STRINGS

LEFT HAND

1 2 3 4

FRETS

NECK

The E-Minor Chord

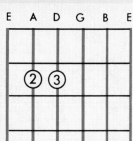

E A D G B E

② ③

When you have learned to play the E-minor chord, you will be able to play an accompaniment for several songs in your book. The chord diagram shows you where to put your fingers on the strings. Press the strings and practice strumming with your thumb.

Using the fingering for the E-minor chord, strum the steady beat to accompany the following songs. These songs can be sung in E minor.

- Yibane Amenu, page 19
- Circles, page 67
- Wind and Snow, page 235

The C and G Chords

These chord diagrams show you how to play the C and G_7 chords.

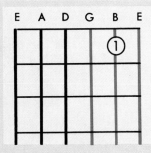 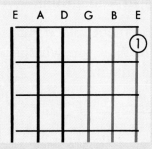

Use the C and G_7 chords to accompany "Annie Lee," page 73.

Try accompanying the round "Row, Row, Row Your Boat" by ear using the C and G_7 chords.

The G and D_7 Chords

Practice changing back and forth from the G chord to the D_7 chord. Then try accompanying "El charro" or "Swing Low, Sweet Chariot." Sing them in G Major.

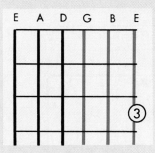 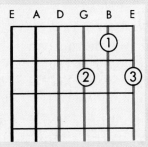

Chord Family of G (G D_7 C)

You can use the G, D_7, and C chords to accompany the following songs in your book.
• Long John, page 106
• Michael, Row the Boat Ashore, page 108

Playing the Recorder

Using your left hand, cover the holes shown in the first diagram.

Cover the top of the mouthpiece with your lips. Blow gently as you whisper "daah." You will be playing B.

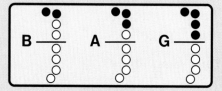

When you can play B, A, and G, you will be able to play melodies 1 and 2.

1.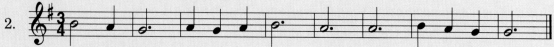

2.

Practice playing two new notes— high C and high D. When you can play them, you are ready to try melody 3.

3.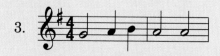

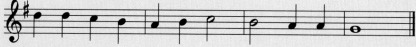

Here are four new notes to practice. When you can play them, you will be ready to try melody 4.

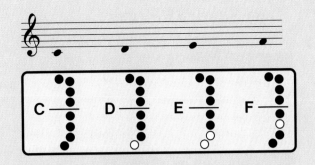

Here are two new notes to practice—F♯ and B♭. When you can play them, you will be ready to try the melody of one of the songs listed below.

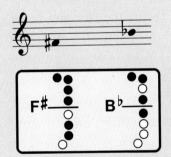

The Sound Bank

Bass Drum A large cylinder-shaped drum. The player can beat one or both sides with a large beater.

- The bass drum has a low "booming" sound, which can be soft and fuzzy or loud and demanding.

Bassoon A large tube-shaped wooden instrument with a double reed. The player blows into the reeds to make the sound and presses keys to change the pitches.

- Lower notes on the bassoon may sound gruff or comical. Higher pitches sound softer and more gentle.

Cello A large wooden string instrument. The player sits with the cello between the knees and reaches around the front to play. It may be plucked with fingers or played with a bow.

- The cello has a rich, warm voice that can sound quite low. Some of the cello's best notes are the ones sixth-graders sing.

Clarinet A cylinder-shaped instrument with a reed in the mouthpiece. It is usually made of wood, but may be plastic or metal. The player blows into the mouthpiece and presses keys to change the pitch.

- The lower notes of the clarinet are soft and hollow. The middle notes are open and bright, and the upper register is thinner and more piercing.

Cymbals Metal plates with hand straps. The player holds one in each hand and quickly claps them together. One cymbal may also be suspended from a metal stand and played with mallets or sticks.

- Cymbals make a loud, exciting crash, but also make sizzling or shimmering sounds.

English horn A long wooden cylinder-shaped wind instrument with a double reed. There is a bulb-shaped bell at one end of the instrument. Pitches are changed by pressing keys.

- The sound of the English horn is similar to that of the oboe. However, it has a lower, warmer range of notes it can play.

Flute A small metal instrument shaped like a pipe. The player holds the instrument sideways and blows across an open mouthpiece to make the sound. Pitches are changed by pressing keys and closing holes in the side of the instrument.

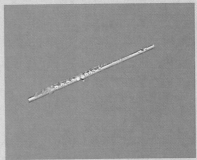

- The flute has a high voice, with a clear, sweet sound.

French horn A medium-size instrument made of coiled brass tubing. It has a large bell at one end, and a funnel-shaped mouthpiece. The player holds the horn in the lap, with one hand inside the bell. Valves on the side of the horn are pressed to change pitch.

- The sound of the French horn is mellow and warm.

Guitar (acoustic) A wooden string instrument with six strings. The player strums or plucks it with a pick or the fingers to play a melody or chords.

- When played softly, the guitar is gentle and sweet. It sounds lush and powerful when it is played more loudly.

Guitar (electric) Electric guitars are flatter and usually made of plastic. They must be plugged into an amplifier.

- Electric guitars are much louder than acoustic guitars. They can make many special sounds with the help of electronics.

Oboe A small wooden cylinder-shaped wind instrument. The player blows into a double reed and changes pitch by pressing keys and covering holes in the side of the instrument.

- The sound of the oboe is thin, sweet, and often exotic. The higher notes are softer, the lower ones more noisy and edgy.

Piano A large keyboard instrument with 88 keys and many strings on the inside. The player presses the keys, and hammers inside the piano strike the strings to make sounds.

- The piano can play high and low. Many notes can be sounded at the same time.

Piccolo A very small flute.

- The piccolo's sound is like the flute's, but higher and more piercing.

Snare Drum A small, cylinder-shaped drum with two heads stretched over the shell. Strings that have been wrapped with wire, called "snares," are attached to the bottom.

- Snare drums can make a long, raspy "roll," or a sharp, rhythmic beating sound.

String Bass The largest string instrument, so tall that the player must sit on a high stool or stand up to play it. The player reaches around the front of the string bass to pluck it or bow it.

- The voice of the string bass is deep, dark, and sometimes rumbling.

Timpani Large basin-shaped drums made of copper or brass, also called "kettle drums." The timpani can be tuned to specific pitches, and the player often uses several drums to play melodic patterns.

- The timpani can create dramatic effects, sounding like crashing thunder, a quiet heartbeat, or marching feet.

Trombone A large brass instrument with a bell at the end of the tubing. Pitches are changed by moving a long *slide* on the side of the instrument.

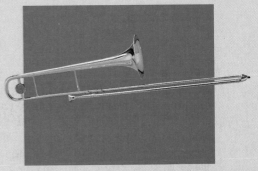

- One of the loudest instruments in the orchestra, the trombone may sound very noisy and aggressive. It can also sound very warm and mellow in its quieter moments.

Trumpet A small brass instrument with coiled tubing and a bell at one end. The player pushes three valves at the top of the instrument to change pitches.

- The sound of the trumpet is bold and bright. On a lyrical melody it can sound sweet, even sad.

Tuba The largest brass instrument, with a very large bell that usually points upward. The player changes the pitch by pressing valves.

- The tuba's sound is very low, deep, and sturdy. When playing a melody, it can sound surprisingly rich and mellow.

Viola A wooden string instrument that is slightly larger than the violin. The viola is held under the player's chin and either bowed or plucked.

- The viola's tone is deeper and more mellow than the violin's, but very similar to it.

Violin The smallest orchestral string instrument. The small wooden violin can make a very large sound when plucked or bowed. It is held under the player's chin.

- The violin can make many different sounds. Its tone can be brilliant, warm, raspy, shrill, vibrant, harsh, or mellow, depending on the way the player uses the instrument.

Glossary

accelerando (p. 160) Making the tempo, or speed of music, get gradually faster.

accent (p. 66) A note or sound that is stressed, or made to stand out.

accompaniment (p. 107) Music that supports the sound of the featured performer(s).

antiphonal (p. 110) "Sound against sound," one group echoing or answering another.

band (p. 138) A balanced group of instruments consisting of woodwinds, brass, and percussion.

beat (p. 56) A repeating pulse that can be felt in some music.

cadence (p. 74) A group of chords or notes at the end of a phrase or piece that gives a feeling of pausing or finishing.

canon (p. 90) A follow-the-leader process, in which a melody is imitated by other voices or instruments, beginning at a later time in the music.

chamber music (p. 39) Music written for small groups, often having only one voice or instrument for each part, as in a string quartet.

choir (p. 129) Commonly used to mean a group of singers, performing together. Also used to mean a group of instruments, as in a brass choir.

chord (p. 94) Three or more different tones played or sung together.

composer (p. 38) A person who makes up pieces of music by putting sounds together in his or her own way.

concerto (p. 48) A piece for one or more solo instruments, accompanied by an orchestra or band, with the solo part(s) dominating the music.

contour (p. 82) The "shape" of a melody, made by the way it moves upward and downward in steps and leaps, and by repeated tones.

contrast (p. 84) Two or more things that are different. In music, for example, slow is a *contrast* to fast; section A is a *contrast* to section B.

countermelody (p. 17) A melody that is played or sung at the same time as another melody.

duet (p. 93) A composition written for two performers.

fanfare (p. 127) A tune for one or more brass instruments, usually short and made of strong, accented passages; fanfares are often used to "announce" someone or something.

form (p. 96) The overall plan of a piece of music.

harmony (p. 86) Two or more different tones sounding at the same time.

interval (p. 75) The distance between tones.

jazz (p. 41) An American musical style made of traditional Western music combined with African rhythms and melodic contours.

lyrics (p. 34) The words of a song.

major scale (p. 75) An arrangement of eight tones in a scale according to the following intervals, or steps: whole, whole, half, whole, whole, whole, half.

medley (p. 41) A group of songs, or parts of songs, that are strung together to make one musical piece.

melody (p. 72) A line of single tones that move upward, downward, or repeat.

minor scale (p. 76) Several arrangements of eight tones in a scale, such as "natural minor": (whole, half, whole, whole, half, whole, whole).

opera (p. 46) A musical play, where most of the "speaking lines" are sung.

operetta (p. 174) A musical play, often similar to an opera, but usually less serious. In an operetta most of the dialog is spoken.

orchestra (p. 38) A balanced group of instruments consisting of strings, woodwinds, brass, and percussion.

ostinato (p. 253) A rhythm or melody pattern that repeats.

overture (p. 174) A piece of music originally designed to be played before the beginning of an opera or musical play, often containing melodies that will later be heard as part of the drama.

phrase (p. 74) A musical "sentence." Each phrase expresses a thought.

pitch (p. 82) The location of a tone with respect to highness or lowness.

range (p. 132) In a melody, the span from the lowest tone to the highest tone.

refrain (p. 9) The part of a song that repeats, using the same melody and usually the same words.

rhythm pattern (p. 38) A group of long and short sounds.

rondo (p. 100) A musical form in which the main musical idea (A) is repeated, with contrasting sections in between (such as ABACA).

round (p. 91) A follow-the-leader process, in which all sing the same melody but start at different times. A round is a kind of canon, but a round is usually repeated (with each voice starting over) any number of times.

scale (p. 75) An arrangement of pitches from lower to higher according to a specific pattern of intervals.

score (p. 110) Written music or notation of a composition, with each of the vocal or instrumental parts appearing in vertical alignment.

step (p. 75) To move from one tone to another, upward or downward, without skipping scale tones in between.

symphony (p. 38) A large, usually lengthy piece of art music for full orchestra. The word is also sometimes used to mean "symphony orchestra."

syncopation (p. 66) A rhythm pattern with stressed notes occurring in unexpected places, usually on "weak" beats of the measure.

tempo (p. 58) The speed of the beat in music.

tone color (p. 119) The special sound that makes one instrument or voice sound different from another.

unison (p. 88) The same pitch.

Reference Bank   265

Classified Index

SONGS

American Indian
Go, My Son *34*

Australia
Waltzing Matilda *12*

Black America
Didn't My Lord Deliver Daniel? *28*
Do, Lord *68*
Ezekiel Saw the Wheel *30*
Let Me Fly *33*
Little Wheel a-Turnin' *31*
Michael, Row the Boat Ashore *120*
Swing Low, Sweet Chariot *30*

Brazil
Tutu Maramba *78*

British Isles
Bonnie Doon *10*
Early One Morning *58*
First Noel, The *234*
Gabriel's Message (Basque Melody) *242*
Holly and the Ivy, The *238*
Scarborough Fair *102*
We Wish You a Merry Christmas *230*

China
Boat on the Lake, A *80*

Czechoslovakia
Waters Ripple and Flow *16*

France
Bring a Torch, Jeannette, Isabella *232*
Ding Dong Merrily on High *238*
In the Moonlight (Au clair de la lune) *14*

Germany
Ring, Bells (Kling, Glockchen) *64*
Silent Night *231*

Israel
Dona Dona *160*
Dundai *76*
Finjan *18*
Hava Nagila *190*
Oh, Chanukah *226*
Purim Day *250*
Yibane Amenu *19*

Italy
Serenade (Lu Lepre) *14*

Japan
Asadoya (Okinawa) *20*

Mexico
El charro *23*
Las mananitas *22*
Springtime (California) *248*

Russia
The Peddler (Korobushka) *17*

Spain
Gabriel's Message (Basque Melody) *242*
When the Chestnut Leaves Were Falling *92*

United States
America *223*
America the Beautiful *222*
Charlottetown *162*
Come, Ye Thankful People, Come *225*
Didn't My Lord Deliver Daniel? *28*
Do, Lord *68*
Ezekiel Saw the Wheel *30*
God of Our Fathers *129*
Home on the Range *89*
Let Me Fly *33*
Little Wheel a-Turnin' *31*
Long John *106*
Michael, Row the Boat Ashore *108*
My Home's in Montana *88*
Peace Like a River *164*
Springtime *248*
Swing Low, Sweet Chariot *87*
When the Saints Go Marching In *87*

West Indies
Hold 'em, Joe *24*
Jamaica Farewell *26*

December Holidays
Around About Chanukah *227*
Bring a Torch, Jeannette, Isabella *232*
Ding Dong Merrily on High *236*
First Nowell, The *234*
Gabriel's Message *242*
Holly and the Ivy, The *238*
Oh, Chanukah *226*
Silent Night *231*
Sounds of Christmas *240*
We Wish You a Merry Christmas *230*
Wind and Snow *235*
Winter Wonderland *228*

Halloween
Halloween Moon *224*

Thanksgiving
Come, Ye Thankful People, Come *225*

Patriotic Holidays
America *223*
America the Beautiful *222*
Away to America *8*

Song Index

Reference Bank 269

Acknowledgments

Credit and appreciation are due publishers and copyright owners for use of the following.

"Barter" by Sara Teasdale, from ANTHOLOGY OF CHILDREN'S LITERATURE. Houghton-Mifflin, 1959, acknowledged to Macmillan

"River Fog" from JAPAN by Fukayabu Kiyowara. Translated by Arthur Waley. Used by permission of Allen and Unwin Publishers, England

"Velvet Shoes" from COLLECTED POEMS OF ELEANOR WYLIE, Copyright 1921, 1932 by Alfred A. Knopf, Inc.

Picture Credits

Contributing Artists: Katherine Ace, Frank Ahern, George Baquaro, Bob Dacey, Helen Davies, Terry Foreman, Glenna Hartwell, Wallop Manyam, Roger Roth, Steven Schindler, Jim Spence, Leslie Stall, David Wisniewski

Photographs: 8: Brown Brothers. 9: E.R. Degginger. 10: Shostal Associates. 13: Steve Jennings/L.G.I. 15: Philadelphia Museum of Art. 16: Jaroslav Kubec/The Stock Market. 20: Honolulu Academy of Arts, Gift of Mrs. Robert P. Griffing, Jr., in memory of Mr. Robert Allerton, 1965. 27: Pictorial Parade. 34: The Granger Collection. 35–37, 39: Mark Philbrick for Silver Burdett & Ginn. 40: Ewing Galloway. 44: Culver Pictures. 47: © Beth Bergman. 56: *t.* Silver Burdett & Ginn; *b.* Ron Scott. 58: Gary Milburn/Tom Stack & Associates. 59: John Gerlach/Tom Stack & Associates. 61: © Martha Swope. 65: *t, m.r.* Silver Burdett & Ginn, courtesy St. Peter's Episcopal Church, Morristown, N.J.; *m.l.* Georges Carde/Shostal Associates; *b.l.* © Noelle Bloom/Southern Living/Photo Researchers, Inc.; *b.r.* © Rigmor Mason/Photo Researchers, Inc. 69, 72, 74–76, 80, 81: Silver Burdett & Ginn. 85: *m.* John Roca/L.G.I.; *b.* David Falconer. 86: David Burnett/Contact Press Images. 87: Margaret Berg/Berg & Associates. 93: E.R. Degginger. 94, 95: Silver Burdett & Ginn. 98: Mark Philbrick for Silver Burdett & Ginn. 106: Silver Burdett & Ginn. 112: E.R. Degginger. 113: Erich Lessing/Magnum. 114: *t.m.* Steve Jennings/L.G.I.; *t.r.* Cheryl Griffin. 116: *l.* The Granger Collection; *r.* Giraudon/Art Resource. 118, 119: The Granger Collection. 121, 122: *t., b.* Silver Burdett & Ginn; *m.* Brownie Harris/The Stock Market. 123, 125, 126: Silver Burdett & Ginn. 127: The Granger Collection. 128, 131, 132, 134–137: Silver Burdett & Ginn. 138: Horst Schafer. 140: *t.* Scala/Art Resource; *b.* Scala New York/Florence. 141: © Eunice Harris/Photo Researchers, Inc. 146: *t.l.* © Lawrence Migdale/Photo Researchers, Inc.; *t.r.* Don Renner/Photo Trends; *b.* Pam Hasegawa/Taurus Photos. 158: Silver Burdett & Ginn. 159: IMAGERY. 161: Stedelijk Museum, Amsterdam. 162: Cheryl Griffin. 165: *t.r.* Merry Alpern/L.G.I.; *m.l.* © Beth Bergman; *m.r.* Nick Elgar/L.G.I.; *b.* © Martha Swope. 166–169, 171, 173: Silver Burdett & Ginn. 184: National Gallery of Art, lent by the Pell Family Trust, Hon. Claiborne Pell, Trustee. 187: © David R. Frazier/Photo Researchers, Inc. 188: New York Public Library Dance Collection. 192, 193: *b.* Culver Pictures; *t.* Brown Brothers. 196, 198: *m.* The Granger Collection; *b.* The Bettmann Archive. 200, 201: © Martha Swope. 221: E.R. Degginger. 222, 223: The Granger Collection. 226, 227: Silver Burdett & Ginn. 230, 233, 235: The Granger Collection. 237: Scala/Art Resource. 243, 245: Silver Burdett & Ginn. 247: Scala/Art Resource. 249: Cheryl Griffin. 250, 256, 258, 260–263: Silver Burdett & Ginn.

5 6 7 8 9 10—RRD—95 94 93 92 91 90 89

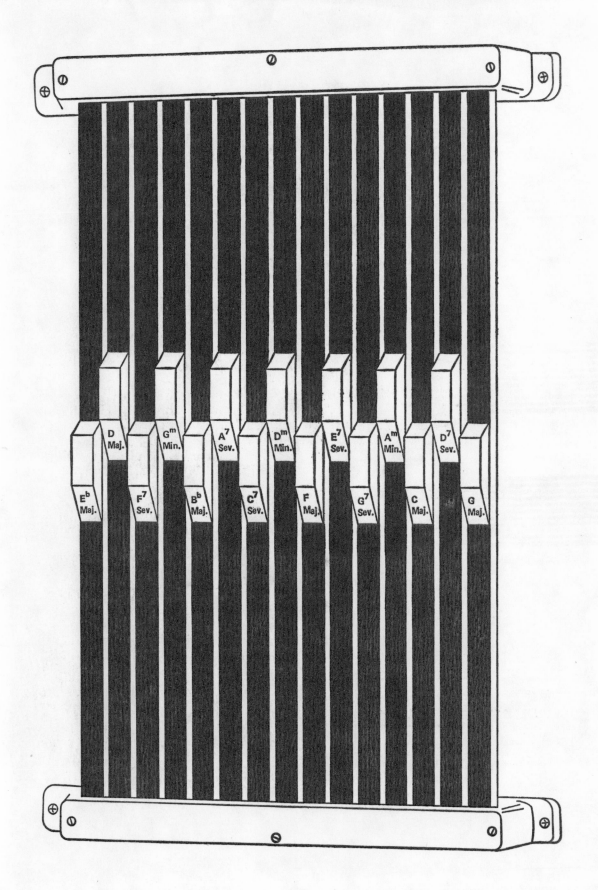